# Iowa

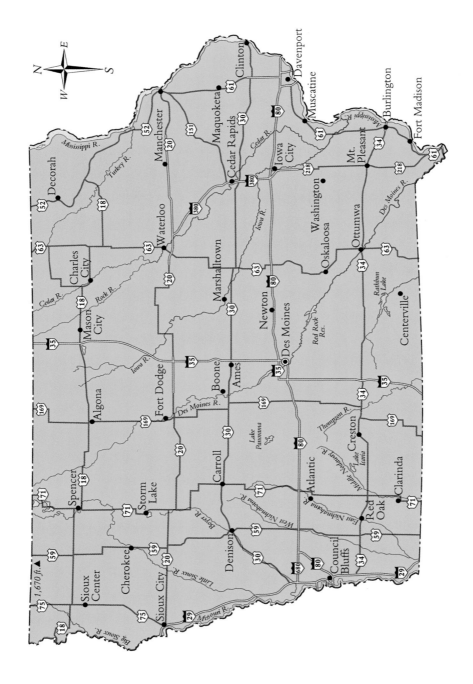

**IOWA BY ROAD**

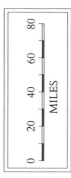

MILES

## Celebrate the States

# Iowa

## Polly Morrice and Joyce Hart

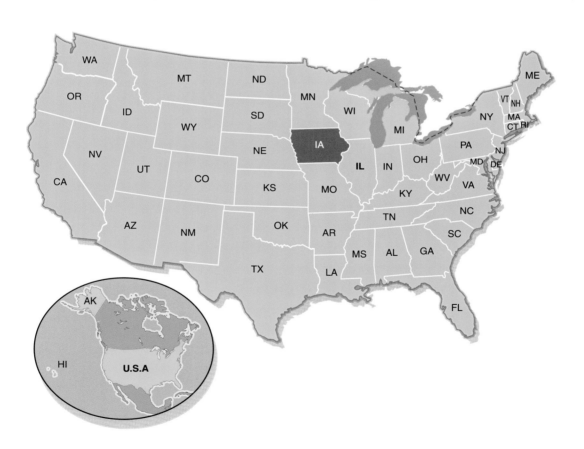

mc **Marshall Cavendish**
Benchmark
New York

Marshall Cavendish Benchmark
99 White Plains Road
Tarrytown, NY 10591-9001
www.marshallcavendish.us

Library of Congress Cataloging-in-Publication Data
Morrice, Polly Alison.
Iowa / by Polly Morrice and Joyce Hart. — 2nd ed.
p. cm. — (Celebrate the states)
Summary: "Provides comprehensive information on the geography, history, wildlife, governmental
structure, economy, cultural diversity, peoples, religion,
and landmarks of Iowa."—Provided by publisher.
Includes bibliographical references and index.
ISBN-13: 978-0-7614-2350-8
ISBN-10: 0-7614-2350-8
1. Iowa—Juvenile literature. I. Hart, Joyce, 1954–. II. Title. III. Series.
F621.3.M67 2007
977.7—dc22    2006013620

Editor: Christine Florie
Editorial Director: Michelle Bisson
Art Director: Anahid Hamparian
Series Designer: Adam Mietlowski

Photo research by Connie Gardner

Cover Photo: Craig Aurness/CORBIS

The photographs in this book are used by permission and courtesy of; *Corbis:* 41, 138; Tom Bean, 12, 17,
63; Phil Schermeister, 13, 137; Michael S. Lewis, 15, 97, 133; Russ Munn, 19; Bettmann, 29, 35, 46;
Historical Picture Archive, 30; Richard T. Nowitz, 49; Julie Habel, 50, 77; Philip Gould, 52; Annie
Griffiths Belt, 61, 98; Tom and Dee Ann McCarthy, 67; Erich Schiegel/Dallas Morning News, 75; Scott
Sinklier, 80, 91; Photocuisine, 89; Jim Richardson, 92; Craig Aurness, 94; Joseph Sohm, 102; Richard
Hamilton Smith, 115; D. Robert and Lori Franz, 117; Macduff Everton, 121, back cover. *Image Works:*
Joe Sohm, 11; Eastcott Momatiuk, 18; Richard Lord, 60; Andre Jenny, 131. Alamy: Clint Farlinger, 21;
Alex s. Maclean, 24; Terrance Klassen, 55; David R. Frazier, 70; Mikael Karisson, 80; North Wind Picture
Archive, 99; Don Smeltzer, 101; Andre Jenny, 107; Robert K. Grubbs, 111 (top). *SuperStock:* Michael P.
Gadomski, 23; age fotostock, 68, 105; Karl Kummels, 84; info a superstock, 111 (bottom); Culver
Pictures, Inc., 129. *The Granger Collection:* 26, 43, 124, 127. *Bridgeman Art Library:* Missouri Prairie Fire
by Catlin, George (1794-1872) (after) Private Collection /Bridgeman Art Library. *North Wind
Picture Archives:* 32,33, 37. *PhotoEdit:* Jeff Greenberg 58; Jim Shaffer, 65. Getty: Brian Bahr, 62; Altrendo
Travel, 106; Hulton Archive, 127. *APWide World Photos:* AP Photo, 135; Charlie Neibergall, 72.

Printed in China
3 5 6 4 2

# Contents

## Iowa is beautiful land . . .

"Taking this Territory, all in all, for convenience of navigation, water, fuel and timber; for richness of soil; for beauty of appearance; and for pleasantness of climate, it surpasses any portion of the United States with which I am acquainted."

—explorer Lieutenant Albert M. Lea

"Is this heaven?"
"No, this is Iowa."

—memorable quotes from 1989 movie *Field of Dreams*

## . . . rich in natural grandeur.

"In Iowa, summer was at its most exuberant stage that the faculties of even the toiling hay-maker, dulled and deadened with never ending drudgery, caught something of the superabundant glow and throb of nature's life."

—author Hamlin Garland

"I remember Muscatine [Iowa] for its summer sunsets. I have never seen any on either side of the ocean which equaled them."

—author Mark Twain

"On the twenty-third we had the quietest and heaviest fall of snow I ever witnessed even in this State of Wonders."

—early settler Bella Williams

"Boy, the wind does blow sometimes! This flat, open ground runs clear to Winnipeg, and God only knows where it ends after that."

—farmer from Peterson, Bob White

## Many people reaped bounty from the land . . .

"At Dubuque in Iowa, I ate the best apple that I ever encountered."

—British novelist Anthony Trollope

"The fertility of the soil of Iowa is unsurpassed—not merely by that of her kindred States—not merely in our Union—but throughout the world!"

—Iowa promoter Nathan H. Parker, 1856

### . . . while others were in awe of it.

"My reason teaches me that land cannot be sold. The Great Spirit gave it to his children to live upon, and cultivate, as far as it is necessary for their subsistence, and so long as they occupy and cultivate it they have the right to the soil. . . . Nothing can be sold, except things as can be carried away."

—Sauk leader Black Hawk

### Iowans are self-sufficient . . .

"What these Iowans don't already have, they figure they don't need."

—character in Meredith Wilson's *The Music Man*

### . . . modest about their achievement . . .

"Iowa has never had the rampant boosterism of Kansas and Missouri. It has always been far too deprecating and self-doubting for that."

—novelist Ruth Suckow

### . . . and proud of their state's possibilities.

"Together we have made a difference. Our community is stronger. It's a better place to live, work, and raise a family, but our work is not finished, for a strong community never stops striving to be stronger."

—Iowa governor Tom Vilsack

*Iowa means different things to different people. Some see its rolling acres of corn, soybeans, and peaceful towns as symbols of a way of life that has vanished elsewhere. Others view its midwestern character and small towns as marks of an ordinary sort of place. The truth is, Iowa overflows with riches: beautiful scenery, friendly people, and festive events. Here is a state where the endless horizon casts a spell. Here is the story of Iowa.*

# Chapter One

# The Middle Border

Iowa is world famous for its rich farmland. "Climb onto a roof-top almost anywhere in the state," said writer Bill Bryson, a native Iowan, "and you are confronted with a . . . sweep of corn as far as the eye can see." Bryson's claim is an exaggeration, but it reflects an astonishing fact: about 89 percent of Iowa's total land is devoted to agriculture. This is more than any other state. The state owes its deep, black topsoil to geology—and to the tall prairie grasses that once seemed as limitless as today's cornfields.

## INLAND SEAS AND GLACIERS

Millions of years ago, Iowa alternated between being covered with warm, shallow seas and being left high and dry, exposed to the weather and erosion. Each time the water ebbed, it deposited sediment—sand and dirt—that gradually hardened into rock. Repeated over and over, this process eventually created Iowa's bedrock: layers of sandstone, limestone, dolomite, and shale.

*In Iowa, corn stalks can grow as high as 8 feet.*

About two million years ago, great sheets of ice called glaciers began to move across the central plains of the present United States. As they moved, the glaciers smoothed the land. They scooped out river valleys, scattered boulders, and, most important for Iowa's future, deposited the soil, stone, and sand that became the basis for fertile topsoil. When the last glaciers receded, about ten thousand years ago, Iowa's basic land shape looked much as it does today.

Some people think that all of Iowa is as flat as a tabletop. However, Iowans know that most of the land in their state rolls gently. From the air, the neat square fields of corn, soybean, and hay suggest a manicured garden, dotted with red barns and white farmhouses. Iowa is a beautiful place. "I feel lucky to have grown up there," a woman from Des Moines once said.

## THE HEART OF THE COUNTRY

Hamlin Garland, one of Iowa's first successful writers, called his state "the Middle Border." The description is fitting since Iowa lies squarely in the middle of the north-central United States. Minnesota and South Dakota form Iowa's northern border, Wisconsin and Illinois are located to the east, Missouri is to the south, and South Dakota and Nebraska are to the west.

Iowa poet Paul Engle once observed that the state has "the stylized outline of a hog, with the snout pushing east between Dubuque and Davenport." Other Iowans argue that, because of the small panhandle at its southeastern boundary, Iowa is shaped more like a miniature United States. Iowa's highest point, 1,670 feet, is on a family farm in the extreme northwest of the state; Iowa's lowest point of 480 feet is at the southeastern tip, near the meeting place of the Mississippi and Des Moines rivers.

*Iowa is sometimes called the Land of the Rolling Prairie because of the rolling nature of the landscape.*

A look at Iowa's regions reveals just how powerful the glaciers were. The northeastern section of the state experienced little glacial activity and is now known as Little Switzerland. Rocky bluffs and cliffs rise abruptly from the banks of the Mississippi River. The cliffs reach heights of 400 feet. Valleys are steep in this area, and trees are abundant.

North-central Iowa, by contrast, is considerably flatter. There, massive ice sheets carved out marshes, small lakes, and depressions that the early pioneers called "kittleholes." When settlers drained the boggy land, they found it contained some of the world's richest, most fertile soil.

*High above the Mississippi River in Iowa, are rocky outcroppings and steep cliffs.*

Most of the rest of the state is covered with gently rolling hills. The exception, which attracts tourists and geologists alike, are the Loess Hills in Iowa's extreme west, which border the Missouri River. The Loess Hills resemble giant snowdrifts of soil. They were created from heaps of silt that were deposited along the Missouri River by the glaciers. When the silt dried, it was then blown beyond the riverbank into the softly rounded hills. These wind-made dunes are found only in Iowa and in some parts of China. The region's early Native Americans considered the Loess Hills sacred.

*In far western Iowa the Loess Hills rise 200 feet above the plains.*

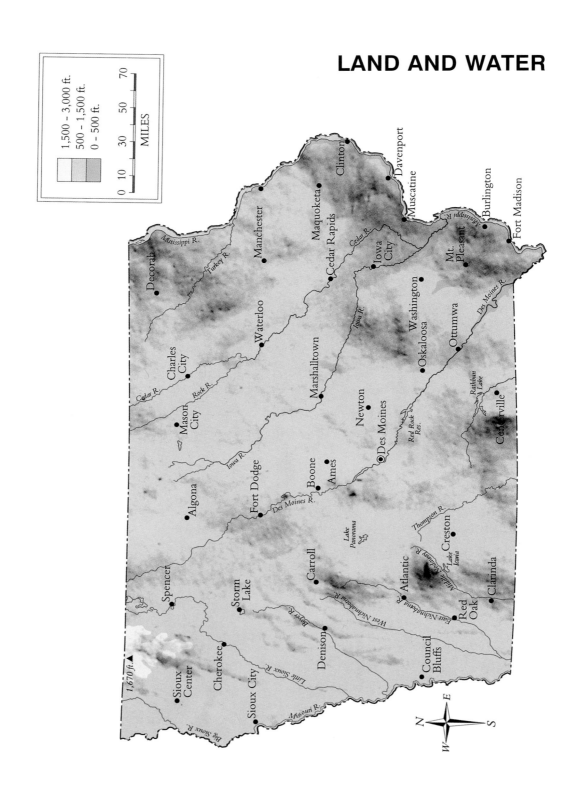

# LAND AND WATER

**Scale / Legend:**
- 1,500 – 3,000 ft.
- 500 – 1,500 ft.
- 0 – 500 ft.

MILES
0  10  30  50  70

Decorah

Mississippi R.

Turkey R.

Manchester

Maquoketa

Clinton

Davenport

Muscatine

Cedar R.

Cedar Rapids

Iowa City

Burlington

Mississippi R.

Fort Madison

Mt. Pleasant

Waterloo

Washington

Des Moines R.

Charles City

Iowa R.

Marshalltown

Oskaloosa

Ottumwa

Cedar R.

Rock R.

Mason City

Newton

Des Moines

Red Rock Res.

Rathbun Lake

Centerville

Iowa R.

Boone

Ames

Algona

Fort Dodge

Des Moines R.

Lake Panorama

Thompson R.

Creston

Lake Icaria

Spencer

Carroll

Atlantic

Clarinda

Storm Lake

Boyer R.

Middle Nodaway R.

West Nishnabotna R.

East Nishnabotna R.

Red Oak

1,670 ft. ▲

Sioux Center

Cherokee

Denison

Council Bluffs

Little Sioux R.

Sioux City

Missouri R.

Big Sioux R.

N
E
S
W

Iowa is the only state bordered by two navigable rivers and the only state with four border rivers. The mighty Mississippi River flows the full length of Iowa's eastern boundary. On the western border is the Big Sioux River, which joins the Missouri River at Sioux City; the Missouri then runs along the remainder of Iowa's western border. The Des Moines River forms one side of the "panhandle" in southeastern Iowa.

A low ridge curving from Dickinson County in northwestern Iowa to Davis County in the state's southeastern section serves as the state's divide. Rivers located to the west, including the Big and Little Sioux and the Floyd, flow into the Missouri. Rivers east of the ridge, such as the Des Moines (central Iowa's largest river), flow into the Mississippi. Each year, millions of tons of cargo are shipped on the Mississippi and Missouri rivers.

Iowa has no large natural lakes, but many of its small lakes are beautiful. In the northwest, glaciers scooped out Iowa's so-called Great Lakes, which include Spirit Lake, West Okoboki Lake, and East Okoboji Lake.

Scattered elsewhere in the state are artificial lakes (reservoirs) created by dams built on the rivers. Many people come to these reservoirs to fish, swim, picnic, and camp. The reservoirs include Coralville Lake, on the Iowa River; Red Rock Lake and Saylorville Lake, both on the Des Moines River; and the largest of all—Rathbun Lake, on the Chariton River in extreme south-central Iowa.

*Spirit Lake is the largest natural lake in Iowa at more than 5,500 acres.*

The first white settlers in Iowa were lured by promises of a moderate, healthful climate. Iowa historian Glenda Riley joked that "maybe there was some logic . . . which assumed that if Iowa was good for corn, it was good for people."

In fact, like all of the upper Midwest, Iowa has a climate of extremes. Its central location makes it a crossroads for air masses and fronts moving in from all directions. The resulting weather can be very dramatic. The temperature can drop 50 degrees Fahrenheit in a single day.

The lowest temperature ever recorded in the state was −47°F, which occurred twice in the state's history. It first occurred at Washta, in northwestern Iowa, on January 12, 1912, and then at Elkader in northeastern Iowa on February 3, 1996.

Harsh arctic winds, accompanied by heavy snowfall and cold temperatures, produce terrific storms called blizzards (the term *blizzard* was coined by a nineteenth-century Iowa journalist). Farmers have planted trees to help break the force of the wind. Still, some blizzards are devastating. In April 1973 a blizzard caused fourteen deaths and $19 million in livestock losses.

During the spring and summer, Iowans witness awesome thunderstorms. From May through August, on average there are fifty days when lightning streaks across darkened Iowa skies. The same conditions that cause thunderstorms—warm updrafts of wind colliding with cold downdrafts—sometimes spawn tornadoes. These powerful "twisters" occur when winds blowing in opposite directions around an updraft begin to whirl violently, sometimes tearing roofs off houses and reducing groves of trees to splinters. One Iowan recalled that after a tornado hit his grandfather's farm near Eagle Grove, the family found a piece of straw driven into a plank of wood on the side of a barn.

Gail Schorre, an architect who grew up in Webster City, said, "I remember going out and seeing the clouds swirling into spiral shapes. It was the most exciting weather."

During an average season, Iowans report about thirty official tornadoes and more than a hundred funnel clouds. Iowa suffers more tornadoes for its area than any other state.

*Warm summers in Iowa can produce fierce thunderstorms.*

## WEATHER EXTREMES

In February 2005, according to the National Climatic Data Center, Iowa was ranked as the ninth driest state in the United States. Later that year, in September, parts of eastern Iowa were declared agricultural disaster areas. But unusually dry weather is not always the problem in Iowa, as the state has also received its share of floods. For instance, in 2004, the president of the United States declared fourteen counties of Iowa major disaster areas after four straight days of rain caused several rivers to overflow, damaging many Iowa homes. Also in 2004 Iowans witnessed a record number of tornadoes (120), and on April 11, 2001, the state experienced thirty-two tornadoes in one day. December 2000 was a very cold month for the entire nation, according to the National Oceanic and Atmospheric Administration. Many cities received record-breaking snowfalls, such as Des Moines, where 26.9 inches of snow fell during that month, and Waterloo, where residents watched 34 inches of the white stuff fall.

By mid-2006 Iowa's temperatures were above average overall and weather experts were predicting some relief from the drought conditions that have plagued Iowa in recent years.

## A LONG GROWING SEASON

Although Iowa's climate can be hard on people, it is nearly perfect for agriculture. Rainy springs combined with long, hot growing seasons (150 days, on average) produce bountiful crops. Iowa's highest recorded temperature was 118°F, measured at Keokuk, on the state's southern tip, on July 20, 1934. More often, mid-summer temperatures hover in the mid- to high eighties. The hot days and nights contribute to successful crops. Even the blanket of snow that can cover Iowa from December until March is useful, because it helps store moisture in the soil for spring planting. It also contributes to the 26 to 36 inches of annual precipitation that fall on the state.

*Iowa's climate and rich, fertile soil support the growth of healthy crops.*

Most Iowans take pride in their state's changeable weather and in their ability to adapt to it. "Some years, on my birthday, there would be flowers blooming," recalled Gail Schorre, who was born on March 28. "In other years we'd have a snow day and miss school."

## FOREST AND PRAIRIE

Before the settlers came, woodlands covered 20 percent of Iowa, mainly along the Mississippi River and around streams. So many trees were cut down to build cabins and to clear land for farming that now only 4 percent of Iowa is forested.

White oak and hickory forests still grow on the state's slopes and hilltops. In river floodplains, cottonwoods thrive. Each autumn their leaves turn a multitude of colors: golds, reds, and browns.

Iowa has lost many of its forests and has preserved even less of its greatest natural treasure, the prairies. In the early nineteenth century, nearly 80 percent of the state was covered by tallgrass prairies. Today, it is almost impossible to imagine the Iowa landscape that was first seen by Native Americans and early settlers. In letters and journals, the awed pioneers described the prairies as "seas of grass." The grass was so high it hid the tops of their covered wagons. In spring and summer, brilliant wildflowers transformed the prairie into "one great flower garden," according to a delighted pioneer woman.

The prairie grasses, such as big bluestem and Indian grass, contributed to the 16- to 24-inch layer of topsoil that so impressed the newcomers. Wayne Petersen, a conservationist with the Natural Resources Conservation Service in Johnson County, said that "Iowa owes its rich soil to prairie vegetation that contributes more organic matter each year to the soil than a forest." Unlike trees, prairie grasses die back to the ground annually and then decompose, enriching the soil.

*Hundreds of species of plants and grasses make up the prairie landscape in Iowa.*

By 1900 almost all of Iowa's great prairie had been plowed under. It was replaced by cultivated fields with ribbons of road running through them. Nowadays, only about 3,000 acres of native prairie are left. Some remnants can be found in ditches or old cemeteries, but most remaining prairies are protected in state preserves such as Hayden Prairie, near Cresco in northeastern Iowa.

Over the past thirty years, some Iowans have joined a movement to re-create the prairies of their state's natural heritage. They have started growing small prairies of their own. Paul Christiansen of Mount Vernon is a prairie enthusiast. "We're throwing away a lot of knowledge if we don't preserve prairie species and their interactions," he said. "It would be like burning a library or museum and losing the information there. Once it's gone, it's gone."

## WILDLIFE

Farming and settlement have also affected Iowa's wild animal populations. The state's prairies, woodlands, and wetlands once teemed with wildlife. Herds of bison, elk, and deer grazed in the fields, while otters and beaver splashed in rivers and streams. Twice a year the skies turned black with migrating passenger pigeons.

Settlers hunted some of these animals to near extinction. Other species vanished when their habitats disappeared. The plowing of the prairies threatened the survival of the prairie chicken. Similarly, when farmers drained swampy land, they destroyed nesting and feeding sites for waterfowl. One hundred years ago, Iowa's wetlands totaled six million acres. Today, only about 40,000 acres remain.

Fortunately, Iowa still provides nesting grounds for many birds, including quail, pheasants, and wild turkeys. Canadian geese are once again nesting in Iowa in large numbers.

By 1900 the white-tailed deer had nearly disappeared in Iowa. The state's deer population now numbers 300,000, but the increase has brought it into direct conflict with people. Each year, Iowa records 11,000 accidents between deer and cars.

*Over hunting and loss of habitat diminished the number of wild turkeys in Iowa. Today, their numbers have been restored through reintroduction of the species to their natural habitat.*

Iowa farmers are taking measures to preserve the state's natural resources. After the prairies were converted to farmlands, Iowa's miraculous topsoil was threatened by erosion. In many places, the original 16- to 24-inch layer has been reduced to 8 inches.

Serious efforts at conserving Iowa's topsoil began in the 1930s. Today, the state employs experts to advise farmers on the best techniques for preventing erosion. Some farmers develop systems of their own, such as building terraces and plowing their hilly fields on a contour.

Iowans are also restoring their wetlands. The Iowa River Corridor Project, funded by the federal government, is re-creating wetlands along nearly 50 miles of the Iowa River. By returning acres of corn and hay to strips of wetlands, the project has reduced flooding and has improved the river's water quality.

*Contour farming creates dramatic natural art and conserves the land at the same time.*

With nearly three million people living in the state, Iowa will never return to the wilderness it once was. But modern Iowans are facing the challenge of conserving what is left of their natural heritage.

Clint Fraley, an outdoorsman and a former member of the Clay County Conservation Board, said that the best way to encourage conservation is to start with school kids. "I just want to get people excited," he said. "You can't force anybody to get interested in anything, but if you once get them into it, get them out on the prairie or into the woods, they might take off on their own and might get really excited."

## STUDENTS TAKE ACTION

In an ongoing project, under the leadership of faculty at Akron-Westfield Community School, located close to the western border of Iowa, students are monitoring an 80-acre wetlands located on the edges of the Big Sioux River. The piece of land was farmed until the 1990s, when it was given as a gift to the city of Akron. Akron-Westfield's students are using the land to study the changes it goes through as it reverts from cropland to wetlands. They check things such as the quality of the water, the conditions of the soil, and the presence of wildlife. Each new class of students compares the previous class's data with the information that they uncover, thus giving them an idea of the changes that are occurring from year to year. This information helps conservationists in the state to better understand the process of how to return other farmland back to the land's natural state.

# Chapter Two

# Becoming Iowa

The earliest Iowans were nomadic hunters and gatherers. Eleven thousand years ago they stalked mastodons, mammoths, and other prehistoric animals. When the climate grew warmer and these large species became extinct, the native peoples changed their way of life. They developed weapons for hunting bison, deer, and elk. Eventually they settled in villages and began to grow corn and squash.

## TRADERS AND MOUND BUILDERS

By 500 B.C.E. prehistoric cultures inhabited Iowa. Among these were the Woodland people, who had mastered pottery making. From villages on the Mississippi River, they traded their wares with tribes from as far away as the Rocky Mountains. Some of the items they traded for were obsidian (volcanic glass), copper, seashells, and flint, which was used to make arrowheads.

The Woodland people were also Mound Builders. Each year families gathered to construct great earthworks—made of dirt and stones—which were used for burying their dead and for other religious purposes.

*Iowa opened to settlers on June 1, 1833. Most were families from neighboring states.*

Many of these low mounds were circular in shape with conical or flat tops, while others took the forms of animals, such as birds and bears. Great care went into creating these works, some of which have survived many centuries.

Other cultures also thrived in Iowa before the Europeans came. The Glenwood people lived in large, sunken lodges in southwestern Iowa. Another group referred to as the Mill Creek people settled along the Big and Little Sioux rivers.

Many of these cultures lived in small bands, or groups. They hunted and gathered wild plants for food. They made tools out of stone, animal bones, shells, and wood. Their clothes were often made out of vegetation or animal skins. Some groups also used animal hides to cover the tops of their huts. As time passed, some tribes settled along the shores of the rivers, using the fertile soil there to plant seeds they had gathered. Archaeologists have discovered pieces of pottery, so they know that these ancient people also used clay to make pots.

During the 1300s C.E. the Mill Creek people, and other Native American cultures that were living in the region that would become Iowa, began to leave. Around the same time a group called the Oneota entered the area. The Oneota people were widespread in what is now called the Midwest of the United States. Archaeologists have found remnants of this culture in what are now Wisconsin, Nebraska, Minnesota, and other present-day states, as well as in Canada. The Oneota, who built villages throughout what is now Iowa, were likely the ancestors of the Ioway, the tribe that European explorers encountered some three hundred years later.

## EUROPEANS ARRIVE

In 1673 the French explorers Louis Jolliet and Father Jacques Marquette set out from northern Michigan to find the mouth of the Mississippi River.

*Native-American guides take Louis Jolliet and Father Jacques Marquette down the Mississippi River.*

After crossing Wisconsin, they launched their canoes into the Wisconsin River and followed it into the Mississippi River. Paddling downstream, they glimpsed Iowa's green, lush hills. "Beautiful lands," noted Marquette in his diary. On June 25 they went ashore on the western side of the river, becoming the first known Europeans to set foot on Iowa soil.

Nine years later, the French explorer René-Robert Cavelier, Sieur de La Salle claimed the entire Mississippi River Valley for France. He named the vast territory Louisiana, after King Louis XIV.

During the next hundred years, few Europeans ventured into the Iowa grasslands. Occasionally, French fur traders traveled west of the Mississippi to trap beaver. In the mid-1700s two new Native American groups moved in. Driven out of Wisconsin by rival tribes who had bought guns from the French, the Mesquakie (Fox) and the Sauk settled along the Mississippi River bluffs, in what is today Illinois and eastern Iowa.

Iowa's first permanent white resident, Julien Dubuque, arrived in 1788 and settled near the city that bears his name today. He was an ambitious French Canadian who had received permission from the Mesquakie to mine lead. Later he was granted a large piece of land in northeastern Iowa. Dubuque spent the rest of his life in what is now Iowa, successfully mining the lead on his lands (7 miles wide and 21 miles long), which extended along the Mississippi River.

*The Sauk and Fox tribes in Iowa joined as allies in 1734.*

## BECOMING A U.S. TERRITORY

In 1803, desperate for cash, the French emperor Napoleon Bonaparte sold all 885,000 square miles of the Louisiana Territory to the United States. The price was $15 million—less than four cents an acre. Through this deal, vast new lands, including the wilderness of Iowa, became part of the United States.

At first, the land that would one day become Iowa was off-limits to white settlers. By order of the U.S. government, all land west of the Mississippi River still belonged to the Native American people. Easterners were starting to become interested in these lands, though. They had read the reports written by Meriwether Lewis and William Clark, whom President Thomas Jefferson had sent out to explore the immense Louisiana Territory. In the spring of 1804 Lewis and Clark had paddled north along the Missouri River, passing the bluffs and grasslands of present-day western Iowa.

*First settled by Native Americans, the prairie provided them with many natural resources. Later, settlers arrived, finding a land unlike anything they had ever seen.*

The stories they sent back east made many people very curious about this newly purchased land. Another expedition that traveled around the edges of the area that would one day become Iowa was led by Lieutenant Zebulon Pike. Setting out from Saint Louis in 1805, Pike followed the Mississippi River north, scouting likely sites for U.S. military forts.

In 1804 U.S. government agents tricked a small group of Sauk and Fox tribal leaders into signing a treaty. On behalf of their tribe, these Native Americans agreed to abandon their lands in the area of what would become Illinois and move across the Mississippi River into present-day Iowa. By 1830 the Sauk people had reluctantly migrated to their new homes, where they planted crops and built villages. But the Sauk did not possess these rich lands for long. Iowa's black soil proved too enticing to white settlers. Soon the battles over these lands would begin.

*The Sauk and Fox were farmers who grew corn, beans, and squash.*

## THE LAST BATTLE

In 1832 the aging Sauk leader Black Hawk (whose Native-American name was Makataimeshekiakiak and who had bravely fought with the British in the War of 1812) led an uprising to regain the tribe's lands. Black Hawk confronted U.S. government officials, claiming that the Sauk's land had been taken away from them illegally. When negotiations failed, Black Hawk organized a band of warriors who were determined to take back their land. The Black Hawk War, as it became called, was a disaster for the Native Americans. More than four hundred Native Americans died, including women, children, and the elderly. Black Hawk was captured, and the U.S. government punished the Sauk and Fox peoples by seizing more of the Sauk's territory—a strip of land 50 miles wide located west of the Mississippi River that the tribe had been awarded. This land was then opened for white settlement in 1833. Land-hungry farmers quickly rushed in.

Soon the government forced the remaining Native Americans to sign more treaties. These agreements compelled the tribes to give up even more land. In 1842 the government purchased the last remaining tribal lands held by the Sauk and Fox. In 1848 the Winnebago people—a tribe that U.S. troops had moved into what would become northern Iowa—were also pushed out of the territory. Less than twenty years after Black Hawk mounted his desperate campaign, the Native-American presence in present-day Iowa was nearly ended.

*The Battle of Bad Axe was the final battle between the Sauk and Fox tribes and the U. S. Army ending the Black Hawk War.*

Once Iowa was opened to white settlers, the newcomers arrived in great numbers. They were drawn to the area by exaggerated accounts of the land's riches. One newspaper promised that those who came "with strong minds and willing hands to work" would be "abundantly blessed and rewarded."

The naming of the state of Iowa is steeped in speculation. No one is sure what the names "Iowa" and "Ioway" originally meant. They may be misspellings of *Ayuxwa*, an Indian word that means "one who puts to sleep" or "drowsy one." Other possible translations are "this is the place" or "beautiful land."

*This 1869 engraving depicts the crossing of the plains.*

## CHILDREN ON THE TRAIL

Many of Iowa's early pioneers were children of all ages, from newborns to teenagers. Older kids had many chores to do, such as herding livestock. Children were often affected by illness and accidents. But kids are kids, and many of the youngest trail riders still found ways to have fun on their trip west. They played tag among the covered wagons, gathered wildflowers, and made friends with children traveling in other caravans. One woman remembered her journey to Iowa this way: "Maybe it was hard for the grown folks, but for the children and young people, it was just one long, perfect picnic."

About one-third of the new settlers migrated to what would become Iowa from present-day Illinois, Ohio, Indiana, Wisconsin, and Michigan. Others came from the South, traveling up the Mississippi River on riverboats, while some crossed the Great Lakes and then set out from Chicago in covered wagons.

Present-day Iowa eventually became the place for immigrants from northern and western Europe to build a new home. Some were fleeing famine in their homeland. Others were escaping political problems.

Most newcomers became farmers. They laid claim to land, paying $1.25 an acre for untilled soil. To prepare their land for planting, a few settlers hired professional prairie breakers, who cut furrows through the dense, tangled roots of the prairie grasses with "breaking plows," huge contraptions pulled by as many as sixteen oxen. In the eastern part of the future state, the settlers built small log houses in which to live. In the west, where trees were scarce, the new farmers used prairie sod to construct homes.

Although life on the prairie was often hard, nothing could stop the flow of immigrants. Between 1840 and 1850 Iowa's population increased dramatically from 43,112 to 192,914. But that was not the only major change during that decade. Iowans also began working hard during that time to become a state.

## THE ROAD TO STATEHOOD

The population boom of immigrants was evident even before 1840, so much so that in 1838 the increase in residents convinced the U.S. Congress to create a separate Territory of Iowa. President Martin Van Buren then appointed Robert Lucas as the Territory of Iowa's first territorial governor. Lucas set up county governments and appointed the

*Pioneers use ox-teams to plow the prairie.*

first judges to the territory's supreme court. Lucas also began building the territorial capitol, a handsome stone building that is now a landmark at the University of Iowa.

In order to become a state, the people of Iowa needed to create a state constitution, a set of laws by which the state would be ruled. In 1844 the constitution was completed and submitted to the U.S. Congress. The next year, President John Tyler signed the bill that would make Iowa a state. However, Iowans rejected the offer and for several good reasons, one being that the proposed state was too small! The new boundaries that Congress had drawn cut Iowa Territory by one-third.

# LITTLE OLD SOD SHANTY ON THE PLAIN

"I've got a little bet with the government," said the homesteader. "They're betting me I can't live here for five years, and I'm betting them that I can." Under the terms of the Homestead Act of 1862, people could claim 160 acres of land for free, provided they worked and lived on the claim for five years. Most homesteaders stuck it out.

I rather like the novelty of living in this way,
Though my bill of fare isn't always of the Best,
But I'm happy as a clam on the land of Uncle Sam,
In my little old sod shanty in the West. *Chorus*

But when I left my Eastern home, a bachelor so gay,
To try and win my way to wealth and fame,
I little thought I'd come down to burning twisted hay
In the little old sod shanty on my claim. *Chorus*

My clothes are plastered o'er with dough, I'm looking like a fright,
And everything is scattered round the room;
But I wouldn't give the freedom that I have out in the West
For the table of the Eastern man's old home. *Chorus*

Still, I wish that some kind-hearted girl would pity on me take,
And relieve me from the mess that I am in;
The angel, how I'd bless her if this her home she'd make
In the little old sod shanty on my claim. *Chorus*

And if fate should bless us now and then with an heir
To cheer our hearts with honest pride of fame,
Oh, then we'd be contented for the toil that we had spent
In the little old sod shanty on our claim. *Chorus*

When time enough has lapsed and all those little brats
To noble man and womanhood had grown,
It wouldn't seem half so lonely as round us we should look,
And we'd see the old sod shanty on our claim. *Chorus*

Legislators from northern states had been responsible for dividing up Iowa Territory. They had hoped to bring two new states into the Union, instead of just one. Since Iowa prohibited slavery, the two new states carved from the Iowa Territory, congressmen believed, would be free states. Northerners thought this would ensure that the country's slave states did not outnumber the free ones.

Adjustments were made, though, and Iowa finally became a state in 1846, but not until its western boundary was extended to the Missouri River. Ansel Briggs was elected the first state governor a few months before Iowa was officially accepted as a state. The state capital remained in Iowa City, the former territorial capital. Later, however, in 1857, the state capital was moved to Des Moines, so that it would be located closer to the middle of the population center of the state. At this time, Iowans also wrote a new state constitution.

The year before Iowa was admitted to the Union, Florida also became a state, one that allowed slavery. The arrangement satisfied some people, since it preserved the balance of power in Congress between states that did not allow slavery and those that did. But it did not solve the underlying tensions over slavery that would eventually lead to a bloody civil war.

## IOWANS GO TO WAR

Iowa was the first free state west of the Mississippi River. It attracted many abolitionists—people who worked to end slavery. Many Iowans participated in the Underground Railroad, a system through which people helped slaves secretly flee to the North or to Canada, where they would be free.

When the Civil War broke out in 1861, Iowa quickly rallied to the Union, or Northern, cause. During the four-year conflict, nearly

80,000 Iowans joined the army. Almost one in six of them died; another 8,500 were seriously wounded.

Back home, Iowan women supported their families and organized relief efforts. In Tama County, Marjorie Ann Rogers taught herself to drive a team of horses and to bring farm produce to market, chores that had traditionally been done by men. Once, some men tried to help Rogers down from her wagon. She recalled that she "declined their kindness and said I would get down the same as a man if I could do a man's work."

The war brought other changes to Iowa, some in the political environment of the state. In the mid-1850s Iowans had begun supporting the new Republican Party because it was the antislavery party. After the war, Iowa became almost exclusively Republican in its politics. Its reputation as a one-party state lasted more than a hundred years.

*During the first year of the Civil War, Iowa's 1st Regiment battled Confederate forces at the Battle of Wilson's Creek.*

The war also affected Iowa's economy. The early settlers had been subsistence farmers, meaning they grew or made everything they needed. But during the war, many Iowans became commercial farmers. This means they grew or raised more than they needed and then sold the extra produce. Despite poor transportation during the war, Iowa's farmers were able to supply huge amounts of food to the Union Army.

In the mid-1800s, as farmers were changing from just surviving to actually making a profit, the main crops they were growing included wheat and corn. Much of the corn was fed to the hogs to fatten them up so the farmers could make more money when they sold them. Wheat was grown mostly to sell at the market. Potatoes, however, were a staple food that was eaten by the farmer's family at almost every meal.

## RAILROADS AND GRANGERS

Iowa's first railroad was completed in 1855. It ran between the Mississippi River towns of Muscatine and Davenport, a distance of 30 miles. By 1880 five major lines cut west across the state. The railroads gave Iowa farmers access to markets all across the nation.

By 1870 Iowa led the nation in the production of corn and was second in the number of hogs raised. Railroads helped farmers make more money in some ways, but sometimes the railroads also threatened the farmers' livelihoods. The railroad companies had a monopoly on the prices they charged for shipping freight and carrying passengers. This means that because they had no competition (no other companies offered lower prices), the railroads could charge whatever prices they liked. Often these prices were unreasonably high, causing the farmers hardship. Produce had to be shipped out, and the railroads were the best transportation system to do this because they were fast and efficient. However, the high cost for that transportation took away a lot of the profits that the farmers could have been making on their crops.

To gain a stronger voice in government in order to force the railroads to charge fair prices, many farmers came together and formed the Grange (sometimes called the Patrons of Husbandry). The first Grange

*The Grange Movement gained momentum when it sought the support of the government to regulate shipping prices.*

in Iowa was formed in Newton in 1868. Iowa's Grangers demanded that the state set maximum prices that the railroads could charge. In 1874 the state legislature passed the so-called Granger Laws, which set up a state railroad commission. This commission was supposed to study the farmers' complaints about what the railroads were charging. Unfortunately for the farmers, however, the commission was controlled by the railroads. This, of course, meant that the commission had no power to make any changes in the farmers' favor. Another fifteen years passed before real, effective railway regulations took effect, under the leadership of Governor William Larrabee, the thirteenth governor of Iowa, who sought to extend the government's power to regulate business.

## WILLIAM LARRABEE

William Larrabee, who owned one of the largest private libraries in Iowa during his life, wrote a book in 1893 called *The Railroad Question—A Historical and Practical Treatise on Railroads, and Remedies for Their Abuses*. This book was read by people all over the United States and was even used as a textbook in colleges to help students understand the issues surrounding the railroads. After he retired from the Iowa governorship in 1890, Larrabee spent the rest of his life at his private residence called Montauk, located in Clermont, which is now open for public tours.

## POPULATION GROWTH: 1850–2000

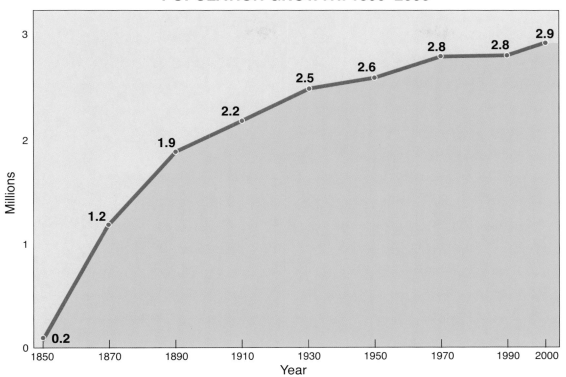

## THE TWENTIETH CENTURY

By 1900 most Iowans were earning a comfortable living from agriculture. During the century's first two decades, corn prices rose, causing land values to soar from an average of $43 an acre in 1900 to an average of $255 an acre twenty years later.

Unfortunately, prices for farm produce dropped abruptly not much later. The 1920s brought hard times to farmers in Iowa and across the country. In October 1929 the stock market crashed, plunging the entire country into the Great Depression. For Iowa farmers, matters grew desperate.

*An Iowa farm is put up for auction during the Great Depression.*

They were forced to sell their corn for ten cents a bushel—less than farmers had received for their corn all the way back in 1857! Because money was so hard to come by, tensions among farmers began to grow. Farmers went on strike and blocked roads that led into some of Iowa's big cities. They would not allow trucks carrying produce to take their goods to the market. In some cases, if the drivers of the trucks did not turn around and go back the way they came, the striking farmers would dump all the produce off their trucks, sometimes spilling hundreds of gallons of milk. The striking farmers believed that by doing this, people would become more aware of how much the farmers were suffering from the low prices.

However, not all of Iowa's farmers approved of the dumping of produce. They believed this was wasteful. Because not all of Iowa's farmers were united in this effort, the farmers' strike did not bring about much relief for anyone. In 1933, however, as part of President Franklin Roosevelt's plan to help free the nation from the effects of the Great Depression, a bill to help farmers during difficult times was signed into law. Henry A. Wallace, an Iowan, was the U.S. secretary of agriculture and was responsible for creating this bill. Although the new bill helped Iowa farmers a little, it was not until the 1940s that they finally recovered from the financial hardships of the Great Depression.

In the years that followed World War II, Iowans began to move off the farms. In 1960, for the first time, more Iowans were living in urban areas than in rural ones. By 2005 over 60 percent of Iowa's population lived in an urban setting. The state's economy, however, still depends on industries that are related to agriculture, such as meatpacking, food processing, and farm-machinery manufacture. Even though fewer people live on farms, Iowa's land—over 80 percent of it—is still devoted to agriculture.

Today, Iowa's farmers are represented by organizations such as the Farmers Union and the Iowa Farm Bureau Federation. Iowa's farmers are working not only to raise produce for themselves, their nation, and people around the world, but they are also promoting ways to protect the environment, to create more sustainable energy sources, and even to educate future generations about the process and concerns of agriculture.

As more and more Iowans move off the state's farms, businesspeople and government officials continue to look for new ways to help the future generations. Education is an important matter, of course, and Iowa is working first to make sure that everyone in the state receives at least a high school education. In 2004, for example, Iowa proudly announced that over 90 percent of the state's high school students earned their diplomas. In 2006 Iowa's legislature was working on proposed legislation, referred to as the 21st Century Scholars, that would make it more affordable for every child to gain the opportunity to go to college.

Many Iowans are also looking for new businesses to develop in the state. Iowa's colleges and universities, for example, have developed research programs that are involved with the biosciences. Businesses in the biosciences include those that deal with improvements in agriculture, animal health, and pharmaceuticals (drugs). If students are trained in this field, bioscience businesses will be attracted to the state and will provide Iowans with new ways to make a living.

One of Iowa's promotional mottos encourages people to "Come Home to Iowa." "The people are friendly, the weather is great, and the scenery is beautiful," reads a Web site that promotes tourism in the state. Another Iowan attraction that many Web sites point out is the state's exciting history, with hundreds of historic buildings, monuments, and sites to remind visitors and Iowans alike of how Iowa began. Iowans will be forever enriched by their colorful history, while, at the same time, they are moving quickly and productively into the twenty-first century.

*At the USDA Research Laboratory in Ames, a scientist collects data on soil samples.*

# Chapter Three

# Ordinary Iowans

Iowa's population has gone through a lot of changes since Iowa became a state. The growth of the population is much slower today and over the years it has fluctuated, rising and falling in waves. From 1979 until 1987 the state's population numbers actually decreased sharply. For instance, in 1986, the state had 37,715 fewer residents than the previous year.

But things are changing once again. More people are choosing to stay in their home state of Iowa, and new people from other states and other countries are deciding to move in. The U.S. Department of Agriculture has predicted that this growing population rate for Iowa will continue at least through 2008.

There are probably as many reasons for living in Iowa as there are people in the state. Iowa's biggest attraction, however, may be the friendliness of its people.

## SMALL TOWNS

In 2005 the estimated population of Iowa was just under 3 million. In other words, the entire state has just about the same number of people as a single

*Iowans love their state and take great pride in its history, heritage, and diversity.*

big city like Chicago. In terms of population sizes, Iowa places thirtieth among the other states in the country. With just over 56,000 square miles, Iowa has a lot of land on which its people can live.

Many Iowans live in the southeastern quarter of the state, but even that area is not densely populated. Resources are distributed fairly equally across the state, with rich farmland found nearly everywhere. As a result, people can make a living in all parts of the state.

Unlike neighboring Illinois, Iowa does not have a sprawling metropolitan area. Approximately 196,000 people live in the capital city of Des Moines. The state's other main urban areas are Cedar Rapids, Davenport, and Sioux City.

Although it has no big cities, Iowa has many small ones. It has sixty-three counties with fewer than 20,000 people living in them. Some people think that small-town life defines the character of Iowa and its people.

*Winterset, Iowa is a small town with a population of 4,700.*

"Iowa has always had a small-town ethos," said an editor of two small Iowa newspapers. "All those qualities that most people associate with rural life and small communities, like openness and trust and a willingness to bend over backward to help others, are still valued here."

The residents of Iowa's small communities tend to be boosters, which mean they like to talk proudly about their towns. They are proud of their environment and seek to share it with others. Billboards across the state welcome visitors to each new town. Some of them read: "Jewel, a Gem in a Friendly Setting" and "Welcome Stranger to Friendly Granger." With the rise of the Internet, some towns have gone online to attract industries and newcomers to their towns.

Not everyone enjoys living in small towns, however. Some people who grew up in small-town Iowa have divided opinions about the lifestyle. Ruth Suckow (1892–1960), an Iowan writer, depicted the state's hamlets as closed societies in which everyone thought alike. For others, however, small towns represent havens where you can know your neighbors and avoid the rush and congestion of bigger cities. In her memoir, *Blooming: A Small-Town Girlhood*, Susan Allen Toth fondly recalled her 1950s childhood in Ames. She and her friends grew up "quietly," she wrote. "We were not seared by fierce poverty, racial tensions, drug abuse, and street crime."

## LOSING AND GAINING POPULATION

During the 1980s Iowa's way of life lost some of its appeal. By 1990 there were 200,000 fewer Iowans than there had been in 1980. Part of the population decline was caused by an agricultural depression. Prices for farm products collapsed, and many farmers lost their land. A severe drought in 1988 intensified farmers' problems. Young people, especially college graduates, left the state to find jobs and new experiences elsewhere.

In the 1990s the trend was reversed. Farm prices were booming again. Unemployment in Iowa was extremely low, and people were interested in living in Iowa again. One major moving company claimed that more moving vans entered Iowa than left it. Between the 1990s and 2006, the growth of Iowa's population, although slow, has continued in a positive direction.

## A MIX OF PEOPLES

Iowans are the descendants of pioneers or the thousands of immigrants who flocked to the state in the mid-nineteenth century. About one in five Iowans has a German ancestor. Other immigrants came in waves from England, Ireland, Norway, Sweden, Bohemia, Holland, and Denmark. All followed the writer Horace Greeley's advice to go west to the "land of the unhidden sky."

Iowa's communities preserve their ethnic ties in many ways. In Pella and Orange counties, which were settled by Dutch immigrants, children receive their Christmas presents early: December 6 is Sinterklaas (Santa Claus) Day, when Saint Nicholas and his servants arrive to hand out gifts. Pella and Orange counties celebrate their Dutch heritage with the Tulip Time Festival, a reminder of the Netherlands' fame for growing tulips. During this time gardens bloom with the vivid flowers and families wear Dutch costumes, complete with wooden shoes.

Decorah, in northeastern Iowa, preserves its Norwegian flavor at the Vesterheim (which means "western home") Norwegian-American Museum, one of the oldest and largest immigrant museums in the country. The museum buildings date from the town's days as a gateway for Norwegian settlers streaming into the American West.

On the other side of the state, Kimballton honors its Danish settlers by flying the U.S. and Danish flags side by side, while nearby Elk

*Pella celebrates its Dutch heritage with a parade at the Tulip Time Festival.*

Horn boasts a windmill that was transported in 30,000 pieces from Denmark and then reassembled.

Iowa's African-American population is concentrated in the cities, particularly Des Moines and Sioux City. The African Americans who came to Iowa in the nineteenth century often worked in the river towns of Keokuk, Burlington, Dubuque, and Muscatine. Others were brought in to work in the coal mines of southern Iowa when other miners went on strike. One very famous African American, George Washington Carver, was a scientist who revolutionized the southern agricultural economy by discovering hundreds of ways to use peanuts, and other southern crops. He studied at Simpson College and Iowa State Agricultural College (now Iowa State University). Carver had been born the son of slaves in Missouri.

# ETHNIC IOWA

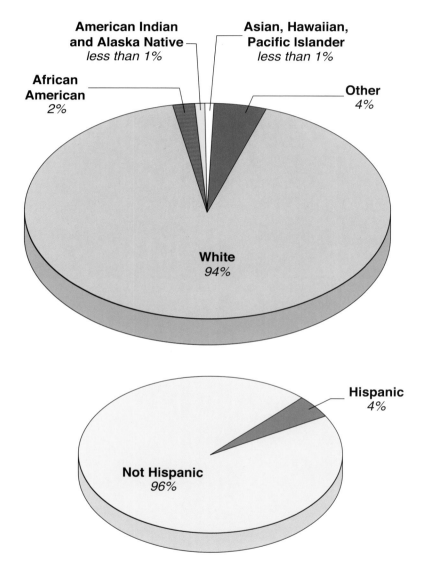

**American Indian and Alaska Native**
*less than 1%*

**Asian, Hawaiian, Pacific Islander**
*less than 1%*

**African American**
2%

**Other**
4%

**White**
94%

**Hispanic**
4%

**Not Hispanic**
96%

*Note: A person of Cuban, Mexican, Puerto Rican, South or Central American, or other Spanish culture or origin, regardless of race, is defined as Hispanic.*

In 1875 steamboats passing through Iowa's waters were forbidden to allow segregation. By 1884 laws in Iowa prohibited segregation of the races. This does not mean that Iowa escaped problems between white Iowans and black Iowans. Compared to some other states, however, Iowa's racial challenges were mild.

Iowa's African-American community has played a role in the state's history that is much bigger than its small size. Iowa's public schools, for instance, were integrated in 1868, when the state supreme court ruled that African-American student Susan Clark could attend Muscatine's public schools. The suit was brought by her father, Alexander, the son of a freed slave who had become a barber. In Des Moines, an African-American newspaper, the *Iowa State Bystander*, was published from 1894 until the mid-1980s.

In 1995 LaMetta K. Wynn made Iowa history by being elected mayor of Clinton, a city on the Mississippi River. She was the first black woman to become mayor of an Iowa town.

Although Iowa was once home to about twenty Native-American tribes, currently there is only one tribe that is officially recognized in Iowa. In the 1850s a group of Mesquakie people who had been forced to live on a Kansas reservation resolved to return to their old territory in Iowa. Using money they had received for moving to Kansas, the Mesquakie purchased 84 acres of land near the present-day town of Tama—paying six times the rate that white settlers would have paid for the same land at the time.

For ten years, the Mesquakie struggled to make a living off their land. They could buy no more land to hunt or to raise crops on, because the federal government had stopped the payments they were receiving while living in Kansas. In 1866 James Harlan, the U.S. secretary of the interior—an Iowan himself—reinstated the payments.

The Mesquakie then acquired a total of 4,300 acres. Today, about six thousand of their descendants remain on this land. Including members of other tribes, there are about 12,000 Native Americans living in Iowa today.

*A Mesquakie tribe member works the tribe's land.*

# POPULATION DENSITY

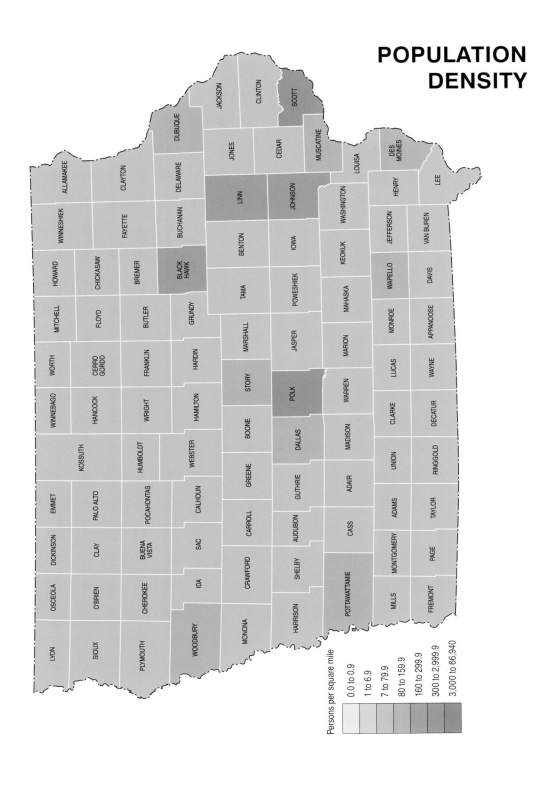

Persons per square mile

0.0 to 0.9
1 to 6.9
7 to 79.9
80 to 159.9
160 to 299.9
300 to 2,999.9
3,000 to 66,940

## NEWCOMERS

Some of the newest Iowans belong to the state's Hispanic community, which is more than 100,000 strong. Hispanics represent the fastest-growing minority in Iowa. Some of the first Hispanics arrived in the early 1940s as migrant workers, who worked on truck farms in eastern Iowa. Over the years, people from a Spanish-speaking, or Hispanic, heritage have come to Iowa from other U.S. states and from places such as Puerto Rico, Cuba, Mexico, and countries in South and Central America. Today there is a large Hispanic population living in Iowa's urban areas, such as Sioux City, Waterloo, and Cedar Rapids. Some Hispanics find jobs in manufacturing, while others run their own businesses. In 2004 Hispanics made up 3.7 percent of the Iowan population.

Other immigrants who have settled in Iowa over the years include Bosnians who came to the United States to escape from war in their country in the 1990s. Like thousands of immigrants before them, the Bosnians were very glad to have reached Iowa. "They hope to make it their home," said Almir Pajazetovic, the group's spokesperson.

According to the 2004 American Community Survey, people living in Iowa who claimed Asian descent numbered about 35,000, while more than a thousand people of Hawaiian or other Pacific Island descent called Iowa home. In Iowa, many cultures are well represented, giving Iowans a chance to learn from one another's different backgrounds. For example, Iowa has many Cambodian residents and more Hmong people from Southeast Asia than any other state.

*Iowa has welcomed Southeast Asians to the state, helping thousands of refugees relocate and begin a new life.*

## THE WILD PRAIRIE ROSE

The Winnebago Indians lived in Iowa in the 1840s. After a few years, the U.S. Army moved them out of the state. This Winnebago folktale explains the origin of Iowa's state flower, the wild prairie rose.

*Long ago, no flowers bloomed on the prairie. The Earth Mother felt very sad when she looked upon her robe of dull shrubs and green grasses.*

*But Earth had many flowers in her heart. One by one, these flowers went out and tried to live upon the prairie. But, each time, the Wind Demon rushed at them and blew out their lives. At last, the Prairie Rose offered to go and bloom upon the colorless prairie.*

*As before, the Wind Demon ran after Prairie Rose. He meant to kill her, too. But when he drew closer, he was charmed by her wonderful fragrance.*

*So the Wind Demon allowed the Prairie Rose to live. Soon he changed and became quiet. He sent gentle breezes over the prairie grasses. The other flowers came up from the heart of the Earth Mother, and her robe became beautiful.*

*Sometimes, the Wind becomes loud and noisy. But this loudness does not last long. And he does not harm a person whose robe is the color of Prairie Rose.*

## SPORTS

Iowa does not have a large enough population base to support major-league sports teams, but sports enthusiasts can enjoy college and high school sports of all kinds. University of Iowa fans focus their attention on the Hawkeyes, who play in the very competitive Big Ten athletic conference. In small towns, residents can track the progress of their high school heroes on the football and baseball fields, as well as on the basketball court.

Girls' sports draw their share of the attention. The popularity of Iowa girls' basketball has even been recognized by the Smithsonian Institution in Washington, D.C. The state also has the Iowa Girls High School Athletic Union, the only organization in the nation devoted solely to interscholastic competition for girls, with more than 70,000 students participating.

*The Iowa Hawkeyes celebrate their win against the Ohio State Buckeyes during the March 2006 Big Ten Tournament.*

## WHEELING IT IN IOWA

Iowa's gently rolling terrain is ideal for bicycling. Each spring and summer, towns and counties across the state sponsor dozens of bicycle races, ranging from the Tour de Poweshiek (in Poweshiek County) to the Snake Alley Criterium in Burlington.

The biggest ride of all is the (Des Moines) *Register*'s Annual Great Bicycle Ride Across Iowa, from the western border to the Mississippi River in the East. This seven-day, 472-mile event attracts thousands of participants from all states, as well as other countries.

Iowa's first church was built by Methodists in 1834 in Dubuque, just two years after the territory opened for settlement. Since then, Iowans have followed a variety of religious traditions.

In the 1840s Methodist "circuit riders" traveled from town to town, preaching gospel and conducting marriages and funerals. Thanks to their efforts, Methodism had the largest number of adherents in the state at that time.

Old Order Amish and Mennonite farmers, who had been persecuted in Germany and Switzerland for their religious beliefs, settled near present-day Kalona in 1846. Old Order Amish still live a simple farming life, without cars, telephones, or electricity.

During the early frontier days, Iowa's empty prairies appealed to people who wanted to build a different kind of community, which they referred to as a "utopia." Iowa's utopias were based on their founders' ideas for a perfect society. Some of these utopian concepts included owning all property in common, by all the people. Some groups also supported what was considered a radical notion at the time, equal rights for women.

Towns with names like Icaria, Salubria, and Communia rose from these concepts of prairie utopias, but most of these communities lasted for only a few years. Many of their members could not agree, and constant arguments developed. After a while, these people drifted back east or to Europe or California or into the general Iowa population.

Iowa's only successful experiment in communal living was the Amana Colonies. Also called the Community of True Inspiration, this German religious group built seven villages on 26,000 acres of rich farmland along the Iowa River. The group owned their lands together and ate in common dining rooms.

*An Amish farmer plows his field without the help of modern equipment.*

For ninety years the Amana Colonies prospered. But gradually, the community's young people began to leave. They took jobs in Iowa City and Des Moines, then they came home to show off their new cars and persuade their friends to come away with them. Finally, in 1932, the villagers voted to dissolve their communal way of life.

Despite their short existence, utopian communities made a difference in Iowa. The groups' biggest contribution, said historian Joseph Wall, was to bring in fresh ideas. They gave Iowa "a much-needed ideological diversity," or different systems of beliefs.

## THE ARTS

Iowa has strong musical traditions that have their roots in the nineteenth century. The first pioneers brought with them both their folk music and a love of singing. After corn-husking season ended, young people from miles around went to "singing schools," where they learned their notes and scales from a "singing professor."

Iowa's settlers also established the "barn dance," which was originally held to celebrate the building of a house or the raising of a barn. Pretty soon people stopped waiting for special occasions. Barn dances became events all by themselves.

With other arts, such as furniture making, Easter egg painting, and quilting, Iowa's handicraft traditions remain strong. The first quilts were household necessities in a land with bitter winters. But they also gave their creators an opportunity to express themselves artistically, and quilting bees provided welcome social occasions for isolated pioneer women. Today, collectors prize older or antique quilts, especially those created by Amish settlers.

*A grandmother teaches her granddaughter the skill of quilting.*

There has also been a rebirth of interest in fashioning these beautiful heirlooms. Leona Hershberger of Kalona took up quilting after retiring from the banking industry. She often pieced together about one quilt a month. "At one time I almost thought it was a lost art, but I think it's coming back. The young people are picking it up," she said.

Marjorie Nejdl demonstrates egg decoration at the National Czech & Slovak Museum & Library in Cedar Falls. Using beeswax and dyes, she creates colorful Easter eggs, each one a unique work of art. "I learned to do this as a child from my uncle and my mother," she said. "It was part of my heritage."

The state's crafts held such an allure for one Iowa woman, that she opened a store that specializes in them. Her small boutique is located not

*These Easter eggs are decorated with Eastern European designs.*

in Ames, her hometown, but in Houston, Texas, where she has lived for fourteen years. The store owner proudly answers questions about her wares. There are Amish quilts dating from the 1930s, handwoven baskets from the Amana Colonies, and wooden cabinets painted in cheerful colors and fanciful designs. As she talks, it becomes clear why she has re-created a little bit of her native state in Texas. "I love Iowa," she admits. "I miss it."

For almost seventy years, literary artists who want to improve their writing skills have applied to the world-famous University of Iowa Writers' Workshop. Many young writers have attended this workshop, earned their master's degrees, and then published award-winning novels, short stories, and poetry. One such person is Lan Samantha Chang, who was appointed the new director at the Writer's Workshop in 2005. Formerly, Chang had taught at Harvard University.

Helping to promote the arts in Iowa is the goal of the Iowa Arts Council, whose mission is to enrich the quality of life and learning in Iowa communities by encouraging involvement in the arts. Some of the activities with which the Iowa Arts Council is involved include the annual national poetry contest called the Poetry Out Loud: National Recitation Contest. The Iowa Arts Council also sponsors a Web site (www.buyiowaart.com), where you can find artwork, such as photography, books, and traditional arts and crafts made by Iowa artists. Through this Web site, the arts of Iowans can be enjoyed (and purchased) from anywhere in the world.

Whether it is through the arts or through an exchange of philosophical, religious, and cultural ideas, the people of Iowa—both those whose ancestors have lived in this prairie land for hundreds of years and who have just recently moved here—work together to make their state a great place to come home to.

# Chapter Four

# Governing the State

Since Iowa's territorial days, Iowans have been active in civic affairs. They register to vote in high numbers, nearly 80 percent. When Iowans go to the polls for statewide elections, they participate in a three-branch system of government that was put in place by the state constitution of 1857.

Like the federal government, Iowa's system ensures that power is distributed equally among the executive, judicial, and legislative arms of government. None of these branches can function without the consent of the people.

## INSIDE GOVERNMENT

### Executive

Every four years Iowa voters elect a governor. As the state's chief officer, the governor proposes how funds should be spent, oversees the operation of thirty departments, and takes final action on all bills passed by the Iowa legislature. The governor can sign a bill to approve it, or veto a bill to reject it. The legislature can override this veto if two-thirds of both the senate and house vote to repass the bill. Voters also elect six other state administrators, including an attorney general and a secretary of agriculture.

*The golden dome of Iowa's State Capitol*

*Governor Tom Vilsack strives to keep the state of Iowa economically sound, as well as providing health care and education to all of the state's residents.*

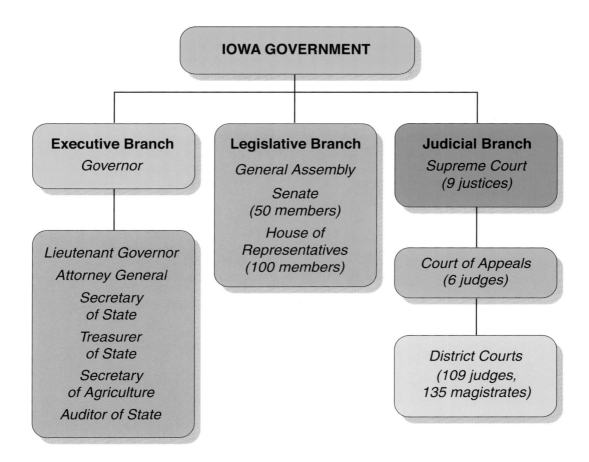

**Legislative**

The Iowa legislature is called the General Assembly. It consists of a senate and a house of representatives. The fifty senators serve four-year terms; the one hundred representatives are elected every two years.

During legislative sessions, members consider hundreds of proposals for new laws and changes to existing laws. These bills can range from reinstating the death penalty to imposing taxes. They affect both day-to-day life and the state's future.

### Judicial

Iowa's judicial branch interprets the state's laws and settles conflicts involving them. The Iowa Supreme Court is the highest court in the state. Its seven members are appointed by the governor but, after the judges have served a year, they must receive voter approval to complete their full terms.

There is also a trial court system whose judges preside over criminal cases and civil cases (in which one person sues another). Cases that involve small amounts of money or minor crimes, called misdemeanors, are heard by county magistrates who are appointed by a special commission.

## IOWA POLITICS AND THE NATION

Iowa may have a small population, but its presidential politics have a national impact. Every four years in late January, a bevy of television and newspaper reporters descend on Iowa. Caucus season has arrived!

Next come the presidential hopefuls, both Republicans and Democrats. They brave the state's wintry winds to address the voters in Iowa at places such as Rotary clubs and political rallies. Their goal is to win their party's Iowa caucuses, or at least make a strong showing.

Political caucuses are basically small meetings. On Mondays in January, groups of Republicans and Democrats get together in public libraries, classrooms, and sometimes even living rooms. At the end of the evening, they vote for their party's presidential nominee. The candidate who wins the most caucuses is the statewide winner.

As the first presidential test, the Iowa caucuses flush out weaker candidates. Because Iowa's caucuses come so early in the year, many national political hopefuls use Iowa as a sort of testing ground to find out how they might do in the national elections that follow in November. Many candidates who do not perform well in Iowa often drop out of the presidential

*Voting takes place during the Iowa caucus in the Madison County courthouse.*

race entirely. Those who rank in the top three to five positions tend to feel optimistic that they have a good chance to win a national presidential election. In 2000, for example, both Democrat Al Gore and Republican George W. Bush won in the Iowa caucuses and then went on to become their party's presidential candidates. In 2004 John Kerry won the Iowa Democratic caucus, prompting some of his opponents to drop out of the national race and significantly weakening his opponents' chances of winning.

Some people think that a state as small as Iowa should not have such a large influence on national issues. They say Iowa does not represent the country's economic or racial diversity. Despite these complaints, Iowa's caucuses continue to draw the nation's attention.

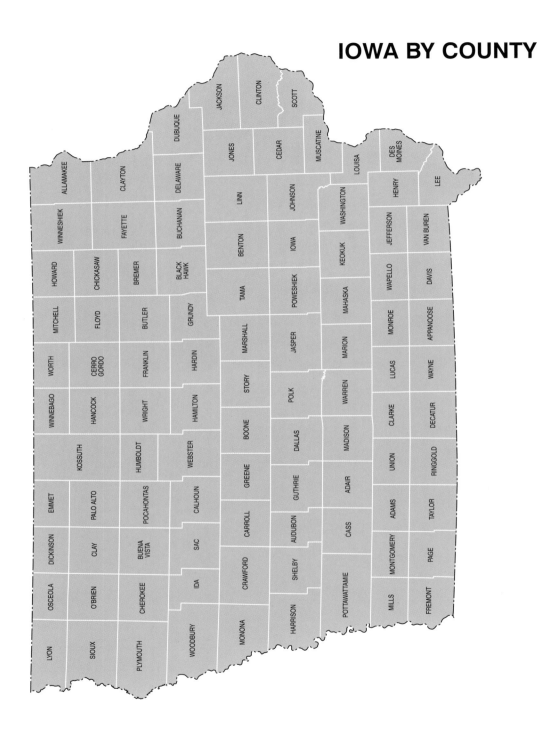

**IOWA BY COUNTY**

Iowa has a long record of looking out for children's interests. Back in the 1890s it was among the first of the states to pass laws regulating child labor. More recently, Iowa set up a child abuse registry. This list contains the names of adults who have been reported for abusing or neglecting children.

Most children in Iowa have access to a good education. In 1838 the first law that the territorial legislature passed was to establish a system of public schools. Because Iowa's population was mostly rural, the one-room schoolhouse became a standard feature of the landscape. By 1937 there were more than nine thousand of them.

*Iowa's Department of Education works to provide a "high quality education system" for Iowa's youth.*

Inside these plain white buildings, one teacher educated ten to fifty children from all grades. Gradually, the one-room schools were consolidated into larger school districts. Farm children began to board buses to go to schools in town. The last public one-room school closed in the mid-1960s.

Iowans are justly proud of their record in education. Iowa has one of the highest literacy rates in the nation, as well as one of the best rates for the number of students who graduate from high school. In addition, the scores that Iowa students earn on college admissions tests are above the national average, as are elementary school scores earned in tests in math and reading.

Helping to further promote access to better educational opportunities is the Iowa Communications Network (ICN), a state agency that provides high-speed Internet, video, and telephone connections to Iowa's public institutions, such as schools, libraries, and hospitals. ICN was funded through a state bill in 1989. By 1993 the ICN was offering services that allow high school and college students to take classes online. Some experts believe online courses help students who might previously have dropped out of school gain their diplomas.

Iowa's public schools do face some challenges in maintaining their reputation. School budgets remain very tight, in part due to a downturn in the national economy over the past few years, as well as significant cuts in state taxes that are normally used to fund schools. When school budgets are tight, there is less money to hire teachers, which increases the number of students in each class. This, in turn, means that students may suffer from a lack of one-on-one attention with their studies. Smaller budgets also can cause shortages of supplies like new textbooks and computers.

In Cedar Rapids, students worry that their schools' award-winning music program will be the first target of budget cuts. One parent warned, "We must be constantly alert to make sure that we do not lose the programs that make our public schools the best in the nation and the world, programs that fill our lives with music and creativity." Fortunately, Cedar Rapids schools can draw on community resources to maintain the quality of education. The Symphony School is a joint project of the public schools and the respected Cedar Rapids Symphony. Symphony members add to their salaries by teaching music classes and providing private lessons. Students, in turn, receive vouchers for symphony tickets, thus promoting and stimulating an interest in music.

## CRIME AND PUNISHMENT

Iowa's violent crime rate is less than the national rate. Many Iowans recall leaving their doors unlocked when they were growing up. How the state should deal with violent offenders causes much debate among Iowans. Some state legislators have introduced bills to reinstate the death penalty, which was abolished in 1965. Their efforts were supported by Governor Terry Branstad, who made the issue of bringing back the death penalty part of his 1990 re-election campaign. State representative Minnette Doderer of Iowa City worked hard to defeat these measures. "We managed to educate people that it [the death penalty] wasn't a solution," Doderer said. "Iowa has one of the lowest murder rates, so why should we have a death penalty?" Iowa's debate over the death penalty is far from decided.

Iowa's state and federal senators and representatives work hard to improve the lives of the state's residents. They do this by making sure that old laws are fair, that current laws are adequate, and that new laws are passed when needed to protect the lifestyle that Iowans enjoy.

*Established in 1939 Iowa's Department of Public Safety dedicates itself to the safety of the state's citizens.*

## THE DEATH PENALTY DEBATE

Since the death penalty was abolished in Iowa in 1965, attempts to make the death penalty legal again have occurred several times in the legislature. So far, all have failed. There have been reinstatement bills passed in the state house of representatives, which have failed to pass in the state senate. In 1998 a reinstatement of the death penalty was again sought by the legislature, but religious leaders and ordinary Iowan citizens influenced the state house to vote against it. Another attempt to reinstate the death penalty occurred in 2006, but it did not receive much attention.

Some Iowans believe that the death penalty would deter crime. Others believe that the death penalty is a way to balance the seriousness of the crime with the seriousness of the punishment. Others believe that the death penalty is morally wrong. In 2005 sixty people were put to death in other U.S. prisons.

Instead of a death penalty, Iowa criminals who commit serious offenses may receive a sentence of life in prison with no chance of receiving parole. Iowa is one of only twelve states (and the District of Columbia) that does not have the death penalty.

# Chapter Five

# Staying on the Farm

Iowa's greatest natural resource is its farmland. Farmers improve on this built-in advantage by relying on sophisticated machinery to plow, plant, and harvest their crops. For instance, the 1920s saw the introduction of hybrid corn, a vigorous, high-yielding plant that resulted from breeding (or "crossing") inbred strains of corn. By the 1950s almost all farmers had adopted hybrid seed, and the state's cornfields produced an amazing one billion bushels a year.

Today, Iowa is among the leading states in growing corn, hay, soybeans, and oats. It is also a major egg and beef producer. Iowa far surpasses all other states in raising pigs: its farmers provide about one-third of the nation's yearly total. Hogs actually outnumber people in Iowa by about five to one (five hogs to every person).

Although farm production remains steady, it has become very difficult for small farmers to succeed. During the 1970s high prices for farm produce caused land prices in Iowa to skyrocket. Then, almost as quickly, produce prices fell again. A U.S. embargo that forbid farmers to export their grain to the Soviet Union made the situation even worse.

*An Iowa farmer inspects the bounty of his autumn corn harvest.*

*Iowa is the number one hog-producing state in the nation.*

As prices fell, farmers who had borrowed money to expand their farms faced enormous debts. Many lost their farms. From 1982 to 1992 nearly one in six Iowa farmers left their land.

In 1990 there were 1,354,928 Iowans living in rural areas and 1,421,827 living in urban settings. By 2005 those numbers had changed, with an estimated 1,340,955 still living in a rural area, while 1,625,379 lived in urban areas. There has been a move away from small towns and farms in Iowa, but don't think that all the state's farmland is being paved over with busy suburban streets. In 2005 Iowa still had 89,000 farms, which covered about 89 percent of Iowa's land area.

## GRILLED CORN ON THE COB

Here's a delicious way to eat corn on the cob that differs from the usual way of boiling it. Hot water can remove some of the corn's flavor. The next time your family is preparing a barbequed dinner, ask if you can grill the corn.

There should be enough ears of corn so each person will have at least one. Remove the husk and silk from each ear, then cut a piece of aluminum foil big enough to wrap each cob individually. Lay the ears on the foil and spread a teaspoon of butter over each ear. Then sprinkle with a little salt and pepper. You might want to add some of your favorite spices, too, such as garlic powder or even a little chili powder. Wrap the aluminum foil around each ear and place the corn on the grill, with your parents' help. In about 20 minutes, carefully remove the corn from the grill (or ask an adult to do so). Open the aluminum wrap, being careful to let the steam inside escape slowly so you don't burn your fingers. Let the corn cool down for a minute or two and then enjoy.

## IOWA WORKFORCE

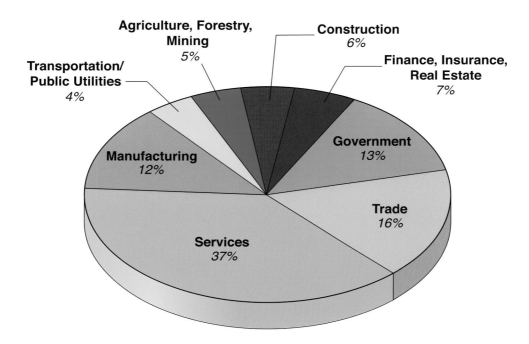

Agriculture, Forestry, Mining 5%

Construction 6%

Finance, Insurance, Real Estate 7%

Transportation/ Public Utilities 4%

Manufacturing 12%

Government 13%

Trade 16%

Services 37%

So, even though some Iowans are moving off farms, there are still many farmers left—enough for Iowa to continue to lead the nation in the raising of several kinds of crops and farm produce.

However, the picture is definitely not perfect for Iowa's farmers. In 2006 fuel prices reached record-breaking highs, which meant that more money was coming out of farmer's pockets for energy costs than in previous years. Added to this were surpluses in grains and hogs, which caused the prices for these farm products to decline.

## A GREAT STATE FAIR

The Iowa State Fair is part carnival and part livestock show. For eleven days in August, thousands of fairgoers from across the Midwest and beyond roam the state fair grounds in Des Moines. Their options range from viewing the Monster Arm Wrestling Championship to admiring the award-winning animals displayed on Blue Ribbon Row.

Many people consider Iowa's version the model for all state fairs. The event dates back to 1854, when it began as a small agricultural show in Fairfield. Since then, Iowa's fair has inspired a novel, three movies, and a stage musical.

Since 1960 Norma "Duffy" Lyon (below) of Toledo, Iowa (known locally as the Butter Cow Lady) has created one of the fair's trademarks, a life-size cow made of butter. In 1996 she marked Iowa's 150th birthday with a three-dimensional butter sculpture of Iowan Grant Wood's most famous painting, *American Gothic*. Before the fair, "Duffy" spends her time in a 40-degree, air-con-ditioned room (to keep the butter from melting), work-ing on her sculptures. Besides the cow, her sculptures have included a motorcycle, a ren-dition of country-western singer Garth Brooks, and the cartoon character Charlie Brown, as well as her very ambitious depiction of Jesus and the apostles at the Last Supper. In 2006 "Duffy" cre-ated a sculpture of famed golfer Tiger Woods.

## 2005 GROSS STATE PRODUCT: $111 Million

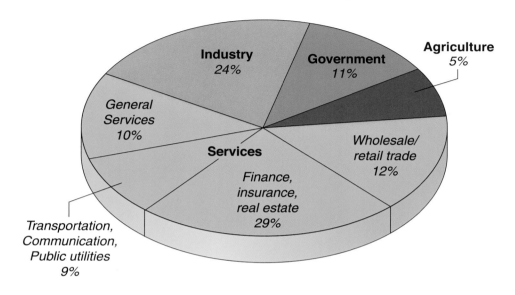

Industry
24%

Government
11%

Agriculture
5%

General
Services
10%

Services

Wholesale/
retail trade
12%

Finance,
insurance,
real estate
29%

Transportation,
Communication,
Public utilities
9%

## INDUSTRY

Industries other than agriculture are gaining in importance in Iowa's economy. In 2004 manufacturing generated over 21 percent of Iowa's gross state product, becoming the largest individual sector of the economy.

Many Iowan industries are linked to agriculture in some way, such as the large factories that process food throughout the state. In Cedar Rapids, the Quaker Oats Company operates the biggest cereal plant in the country. In Sioux City, Waterloo, and Ottumwa you will find major meatpacking centers. The processing of food was the largest industry in the state in 2004. Following food was the manufacture of machinery (which includes a lot of farm machinery), chemicals, transportation equipment, and fabricated metals. Iowa exports many of the materials that are manufactured in the state. In 2005 the state's exports were worth

$7.3 billion, which ranked Iowa as the twenty-seventh state in the value of its exports. Iowa's exported materials went to countries such as Canada, Mexico, Australia, and China, to name just a few.

Although manufacturing provides the most money to Iowa's economy, it is Iowa's service industry that provides the most jobs. The service industry includes jobs in which people help other people. This includes careers such as doctors, retail store salespeople, bankers, waitpersons in restaurants, hotel workers, and government employees, such as teachers.

*A production worker at one of Iowa's food processing plants.*

# EARNING A LIVING

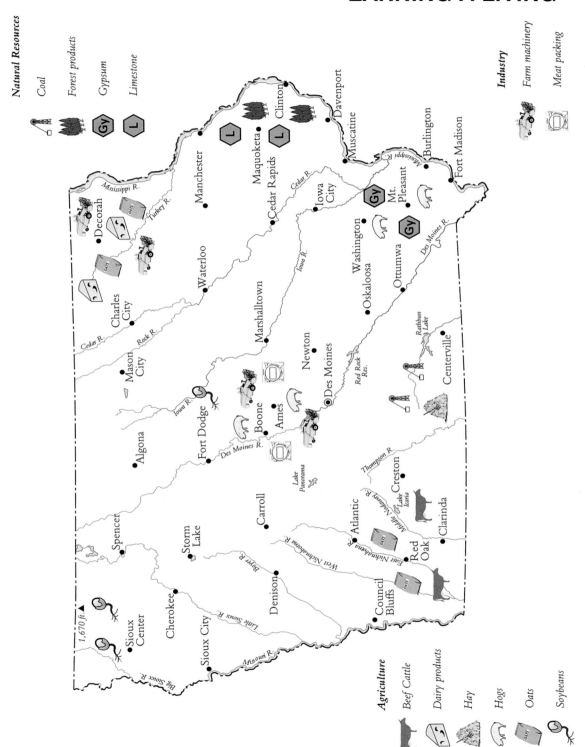

**Natural Resources**

Coal

Forest products

Gypsum

Limestone

**Industry**

Farm machinery

Meat packing

**Agriculture**

Beef Cattle

Dairy products

Hay

Hogs

Oats

Soybeans

Decorah

Manchester

Clinton

Davenport

Muscatine

Burlington

Fort Madison

Maquoketa

Cedar Rapids

Iowa City

Mt. Pleasant

Washington

Oskaloosa

Ottumwa

Charles City

Waterloo

Marshalltown

Newton

Des Moines

Centerville

Mason City

Algona

Fort Dodge

Boone

Ames

Spencer

Carroll

Atlantic

Creston

Clarinda

Storm Lake

Cherokee

Denison

Red Oak

Council Bluffs

Sioux Center

Sioux City

1,670 ft.

Mississippi R.

Turkey R.

Cedar R.

Iowa R.

Rock R.

Cedar R.

Des Moines R.

Iowa R.

Red Rock Res.

Rathbun Lake

Thompson R.

Lake Icaria

Middle Nodaway R.

West Nishnabotna R.

East Nishnabotna R.

Boyer R.

Little Sioux R.

Big Sioux R.

Missouri R.

Lake Panorama

## LOOKING TOWARD THE FUTURE

During the farm depression of the 1980s, many of Iowa's young people left the state, seeking jobs and better futures elsewhere. Many young Iowans appreciate the lifestyle and environment that their state offers. If they could earn a decent wage and find jobs that suit their skills, many people believe these high school and college graduates would happily remain in Iowa. Today, businesspeople, educators, and state government officials are sharing ideas about how to keep young people in Iowa and how to bring back those who have left home.

*Today, Iowa is working hard to keep their young from leaving the state by creating more jobs.*

*This woman works in a seed bank, maintaining thousands of crop varieties for use and research.*

To do these things, Iowa is diversifying its economy. One new field is bioscience. Iowa boasts excellent research facilities for bioscience at its colleges and universities. In 2005 Iowa had more than 1,800 companies involved in bioscience. Looking toward the future, Iowa State University has organized the Plant Sciences Institute to increase its staff and students' ability to research new ways to use crops, such as for vaccinations against diseases or for biologically based fuels.

As Iowans look to the future, they try to determine where the jobs will be. One organization, called Iowa Workforce Development, has created a table that covers its predictions for what Iowa's workforce will look like in 2012. The organization believes that some of the greatest potential for jobs will be in the medical field (medical assistants and home health-care aides, for example) and in technology (computer software engineers and computer analysts, for example). According to the organization's research, jobs that will be declining include typists, travel agents, and post office workers.

In many ways, Iowa is unique. Its small towns and wide open spaces make the state very different from the states along the Atlantic seaboard, for instance. But in other ways, Iowa is just like every other state in the Union. Iowans, like the residents of other states, are trying to gain the best education they can, to find the most rewarding job, to learn from people of different cultures, and to develop the best environment for their families and future generations. There may be no better place to do all of this than in Iowa.

# Chapter Six

# Exploring Iowa

There is a lot to see, both old and new, in Iowa besides the state's beautiful farmlands. Old-fashioned shops and train depots that have been preserved throughout Iowa attract many visitors each year who like to see what small midwestern towns looked like at the turn of the twentieth century. But Iowa has much else to offer, too. The Hawkeye State abounds with historic buildings and sites, scenic views, and even famous movie locations.

## ANCIENT NATIVE-AMERICAN CULTURE

Long before Jacques Marquette and Louis Jolliet paddled their canoes along the Upper Mississippi River, Native Americans buried their dead on the high bluffs rising above the water. Effigy Mounds National Monument is located near the northeastern corner of the state. The park contains more than two hundred prehistoric ceremonial mounds. Thirty-one of these mounds take the shape of birds or bears. Archaeologists believe these distinctive effigies are more than 1,400 years old.

On a bluff overlooking the conjunction of the Iowa and Mississippi rivers, there is another set of mounds that date back to between 100 B.C.E.

*From farms to small towns, historic sites and waterways, there is much to see in Iowa.*

**95**

and 200 C.E. The mounds at the Toolesboro site are considered to be burial mounds of the ancient Hopewell people. There are seven mounds remaining. Two of them can be found outside the Educational Center at Toolesboro. The other five mounds have been protected from the public in order to preserve them. One of the protected mounds may be the largest Hopewell mound in Iowa, measuring 100 feet in diameter and 8 feet in height.

## LIFE ON THE MISSISSIPPI

Steep hills and Victorian houses give Dubuque some of the same charm that the city of San Francisco, in California, has. Dubuque is a picturesque city of more than 57,000 people, and is steeped in midwestern history. To mark some of that history, a monument stands just south of the city, over the grave of Julien Dubuque, the town's namesake. Julien Dubuque was a lead miner, but when the mines were exhausted, the city became a busy lumber town and bustling river port. Relics of the city's colorful past are on display in the National Mississippi River Museum. Here you can learn about explorers, pilots, and riverboat gamblers.

South of Dubuque lie Saint Donatus, which was founded by immigrants from the tiny European nation of Luxembourg. Each year on Good Friday, hundreds of people make their way uphill to the Chapel on the Mount, which is modeled after a chapel in their native country.

About halfway down Iowa's eastern border is the town of Davenport, which has preserved the town's past as a limestone exporter and river port in the Putnam Museum. The Putnam Museum is one of the oldest museums west of the Mississippi.

The "Crookedest Street in the World" (according to Ripley's Believe It or Not) is a steep, zigzagging road in Burlington, Iowa. Built in 1894 Snake Alley makes five half-curves and two quarter-curves in

*The Julien Dubuque Monument*

just 275 feet. Even the bricks were laid at an angle to give horses' hooves a better grip on the slick surface in winter. Every year, determined bicyclists tackle these curves in the Snake Alley Criterium race.

Admirers of Mark Twain will find traces of the great writer's early life in Keokuk. In the mid-1850s Twain worked in a print shop here. Some of his possessions can be seen at the restored Miller House Museum and at the Keokuk Public Library.

Just outside Dyersville lies one of the world's most famous cornfields. Fans of the movie *Field of Dreams* can play a few innings on the baseball diamond featured in the film. There is even a concession stand.

Readers of Laura Ingalls Wilder's *Little House* books like to visit the town of Burr Oak. In the 1870s a plague of grasshoppers destroyed Laura's father, Charles Ingalls's crops in neighboring Minnesota. He moved his family to Burr Oak and tried his hand at the hotel business for a year. A guide takes you through the modest eleven-room hotel that the Ingalls girls and their mother helped to run.

About 30 miles west of Burr Oak stands Hayden Prairie. These 240 acres make up one of the few native prairies left in the state. The spring and fall, when the wildflowers bloom, are the best times to visit—and to imagine how much of Iowa looked when 80 percent of the state was covered with tallgrass prairie.

*Visitors can play ball on the* Field of Dreams *movie site.*

## THE MORMONS' CROSSINGS

Southern Iowa still bears the marks of a remarkable human migration. From 1846 to 1856 as many as 30,000 Mormons crossed the state. Most were on their way to Salt Lake City, Utah, fleeing from Nauvoo, Illinois, where their original leader, Joseph Smith, had been murdered by hostile neighbors.

The first group of emigrants blazed a trail. They established stopping places, planting gardens and digging wells for the thousands of fellow Mormons, naming themselves the Camp of Israel, who would follow them later. Heavy wagon wheels eventually wore down the earth along the Mormon Trail. Remnants of this trail can still be seen from Fort Madison to Council Bluffs.

Some of the crossings took place in howling winter weather. At Mount Pisgah in Union County, thousands of graves bear silent witness to the travelers' hardships. The last wave of Mormons crossed Iowa in 1856.

Thirteen hundred converts from Europe arrived in Iowa City by train and continued across the state on foot. Historians call this the Handcart Expedition because the immigrants pushed or pulled their belongings in carts. Some of these pioneers left the trail and settled in south-central Iowa. Graceland College, in Lamoni, was founded by Mormons who broke with their leader, Brigham Young, and did not follow him all the way to Utah.

In 1891 an American friend of Bohemian composer Antonín Dvořák persuaded him to come to New York City to teach. Dvořák went in 1892 but soon grew homesick for the customs and people of his native land. He spent the summer of 1893 in tiny Spillville, Iowa, founded by immigrants from Bohemia.

In Spillville, Dvořák finished his most famous work, the New World Symphony. Visitors to Spillville can tour the two-story house where Dvořák lived. Upstairs in this house is a museum dedicated to him. The lower floor contains the Bily Clocks Museum, which has a collection of hand-carved timepieces.

The Czech influence is also strong in Cedar Rapids. For many years, Iowa's second-largest city had the highest percentage of Czech residents of any city in the country. In 1995 the building of the National Czech & Slovak Museum & Library was dedicated in Cedar Rapids. The ceremony brought together the presidents of the United States, the Czech Republic, and the Slovak Republic. "Many of our fellow countrymen eventually settled here in Cedar Rapids," said Czech president Václav Havel. "They came here to Iowa to find freedom, prosperity, and mutual tolerance."

The Cedar Rapids Museum of Art contains the world's largest collection of paintings by artist Grant Wood, who spent most of his adult life in Cedar Rapids. In addition, the museum features many works by Marvin Cone, a lifelong friend of Wood's who also painted landscapes of rolling midwestern farmland.

The gem of the University of Iowa's campus in Iowa City is the Old Capitol. A journalist for the *Cedar Rapids Gazette* described the grand limestone front of this building, which was completed in 1842, as "a palace fit for presidents." Most of the limestone used in this building was quarried

## THE AMANA COLONIES

The Amana Colonies are seven villages founded by a nineteenth-century German Protestant sect called the Community of True Inspiration. Tourists enjoy visiting this location to see the picturesque buildings and the high-quality woolens and handcrafted goods for which the people of the Amana Colonies are famous. Tourists also enjoy the colonies' large, country-style restaurants that serve up hearty home-style meals. On weekends, these meals also attract many hungry college students from the University of Iowa and Grinnell College.

Serious cooking is a long tradition in the Amana Colonies. Until 1932 the colonies' residents ate all their meals together in communal dining halls. Each kitchen was run by a *kuchebaas* (kitchen boss). When Amana ended its communal way of life, families began to eat in their own homes. "That's why we have these big restaurants here," explained Emilie Hoppe, author of a cookbook of recipes from the Amana Colonies. "Our restaurants grew out of the communal kitchen heritage."

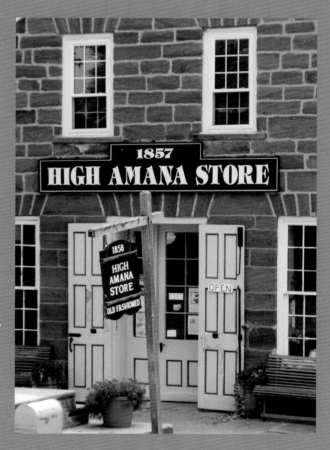

*The old Iowa State Capitol is found on the campus of the University of Iowa.*

from the bluffs along the Iowa River, then floated on barges to Iowa City, where it was pulled by a team of oxen to the site.

In 1857 the state capital was moved to Des Moines, and the Old Capitol was turned over to the university. Today, visitors enjoy climbing the somewhat unusual reverse spiral staircase (which curves to the left instead of to the right like most spiral staircases) in the central hall.

East of Iowa City, in the village of West Branch, is a carefully preserved Quaker cottage. This two-room structure is the birthplace and boyhood home of Herbert Hoover, the only U.S. president born in Iowa. Hoover lived in West Branch until he was ten; after both his parents died, he was sent to Oregon to live with an uncle.

The tranquil grounds of the Herbert Hoover National Historic Site include the Quaker meetinghouse where the Hoover family attended services, as well as the Herbert Hoover Presidential Library and Museum, which attracts Hoover scholars.

*Birthplace cottage of President Herbert Hoover*

# PLACES TO SEE

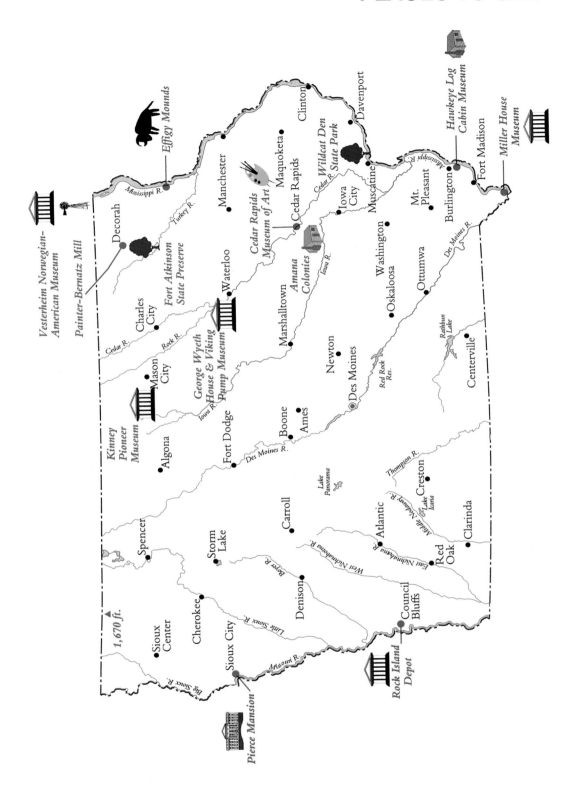

Effigy Mounds

Vesterheim Norwegian–
American Museum

Painter–Bernatz Mill

Mississippi R.

Decorah

Turkey R.

Fort Atkinson
State Preserve

Manchester

Maquoketa

Cedar Rapids
Museum of Art

Cedar Rapids

Clinton

Davenport

Wildcat Den
State Park

Cedar R.

Hawkeye Log
Cabin Museum

Fort Madison

Miller House
Museum

Mississippi R.

Iowa
City

Muscatine

Mt.
Pleasant

Burlington

Waterloo

Charles
City

Cedar R.

Rock R.

George Wyeth
House & Viking
Pump Museum

Marshalltown

Amana
Colonies

Iowa R.

Washington

Oskaloosa

Ottumwa

Des Moines R.

Rathbun
Lake

Mason
City

Iowa R.

Newton

Des Moines

Red Rock
Res.

Centerville

Kinney
Pioneer
Museum

Algona

Fort Dodge

Boone

Ames

Des Moines R.

Lake
Panorama

Thompson R.

Creston

Lake
Icaria

Clarinda

1,670 ft.

Spencer

Storm
Lake

Carroll

Boyer R.

Atlantic

Middle Nodaway R.

Red
Oak

East Nishnabotna R.

West Nishnabotna R.

Sioux
Center

Cherokee

Sioux City

Denison

Little Sioux R.

Council
Bluffs

Rock Island
Depot

Missouri R.

Big Sioux R.

Pierce Mansion

## CENTRAL IOWA

The side-by-side towns of Clear Lake and Mason City have ties to famous musical figures. Composer Meredith Willson grew up in Mason City. He used his hometown as the model for River City, the setting of his hit Broadway musical, *The Music Man*.

In Clear Lake, a monument memorializes the rock-and-roll legends Buddy Holly, Ritchie Valens, and J.P. Richardson, who was better known as the Big Bopper. In 1959, after a performance, these rock-and-roll pioneers were killed in a plane crash near Clear Lake.

Iowa's capital, cultural center, and largest city is Des Moines. The State Capitol rises from a hilltop overlooking the city. Work on this landmark went on for fifteen years before it was finally completed in 1886.

*Iowa's General Assembly meets at the State Capitol in Des Moines.*

In the process, one architect died, one resigned, and the next two encountered major challenges in carrying out the ambitious design. The result is a massive building with a central dome covered in gleaming gold leaf and four smaller domes at the corners.

Iowa has one of the few governor's residences in the nation that are open to the public. Terrace Hill is a splendid mansion, built in 1869 for a Des Moines millionaire. In 1977 the estate became the governor's residence. It is open to tourists from March through December.

The small town of Winterset, in Madison County, was the birthplace of Marion Michael Morrison, who grew up to be the Duke—actor John Wayne. After touring John Wayne's boyhood home, you can make another Hollywood-related excursion. Madison County is the site of half a dozen covered bridges built in the nineteenth century. First made famous by Iowan

*Holliwell Bridge is the largest covered bridge in Madison County at 122 feet.*

Robert James Waller's novel *The Bridges of Madison County*, they were later featured in a movie of the same name. All are open to visitors.

## WESTERN IOWA

Iowa's northwestern corner contains the state's beautiful "Great Lakes." Scooped out by glaciers, these large, clear lakes are popular resort areas. But they were not always vacation spots. In the 1850s the Sioux Indians held religious meetings along Spirit Lake and East and West Okoboji lakes.

In February 1857 a band of Sioux, led by the rebel leader Inkpaduta, discovered that a handful of white settlers had staked claims and built cabins along the lakes' sacred shores. This discovery, coupled with the unusual harshness of the winter, sparked a tragedy.

*West Okoboji Lake is spring fed and 134 feet deep.*

## TEN LARGEST CITIES

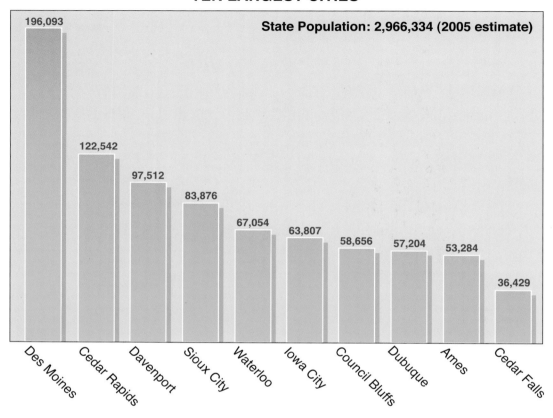

**State Population: 2,966,334 (2005 estimate)**

| City | Population |
|------|-----------|
| Des Moines | 196,093 |
| Cedar Rapids | 122,542 |
| Davenport | 97,512 |
| Sioux City | 83,876 |
| Waterloo | 67,054 |
| Iowa City | 63,807 |
| Council Bluffs | 58,656 |
| Dubuque | 57,204 |
| Ames | 53,284 |
| Cedar Falls | 36,429 |

Moving swiftly from one isolated house to another, Inkpaduta and his followers killed thirty-four of the settlers and carried off four captives. The Spirit Lake Massacre, as the incident was called, was perhaps the saddest chapter in the history of white-Indian relationships in Iowa.

Although a search party set out, it never caught Inkpaduta. Eventually, two of the prisoners were freed by their captors. Abbie Gardner, whose family perished in the attack, wrote extensively about her experience. The Gardner cabin still stands in Arnolds Park, overlooking West Okoboji Lake.

In West Bend, in northwestern Iowa, you can visit a replica of a sod house, the type of dwelling that many pioneers constructed because there were few trees on the prairie. Sod houses were made out of sod—dirt held in the roots of prairie grass. When there were heavy rainfalls there were many muddy places both outside and inside the house. Despite the dirty conditions (and a lot of bugs), there are surprisingly many accounts written by early settlers claiming that these sod houses were quite comfortable to live in because they stayed warm in the winter and cool in the summer.

Sioux City, on Iowa's border with Nebraska-South Dakota, rose to prominence as a meatpacking center, but students of architecture know it as the site of the Woodbury County Courthouse. Completed in 1918 by architects who had studied with the master Louis Sullivan, the courthouse features leaded glass windows and ornamental sculptures in terra cotta. In designing the building, the architects incorporated some of the principles of the Prairie Style, a kind of architecture intended to harmonize with the rolling midwestern prairies.

A different sort of judicial architecture can be found in Council Bluffs. Prisoners kept in the "Squirrel Cage Jail," built in 1885, had no chance of escape. Their cells had no doors! The jail is a circular, three-tier structure containing wedge-shaped cells; ten of these make up each metal floor. To reach one of the prisoners, the jailer turned a crank until the prisoner's cell aligned with the jail's opening. The Squirrel Cage Jail was used until 1969.

In the southwestern part of the state, in the town of Lewis, stands the preserved Hitchcock House, which celebrated its 150th anniversary in 2006. The Hitchcock House, a national historic landmark, was once used as part of the Underground Railroad. Visitors can enjoy special events that are held here each year and can also inspect the hidden room in the basement where runaway slaves were protected on their journey to freedom from the South to the Northern states and Canada.

THE FLAG: *The state flag has three panels, one for each of the state's colors.
In the middle panel, against a white background, is a reproduction of the
eagle from the state seal. The eagle is carrying a streamer with the state motto.*

THE SEAL: *In the foreground a
soldier holds an American flag
with thirteen stars that stand for
the original thirteen states in his
right hand and a gun in his left
hand. A plow, a sheaf of wheat,
and a sickle represent agriculture.
To the soldier's right are a pile of
pig lead and a lead furnace. The
Mississippi River and the steamboat in the background symbolize
commerce. The state seal was
adopted in 1847.*

# State Survey

**Statehood:** December 28, 1846

**Origin of Name:** Possibly named for the Ioway Indian tribe that inhabited this area. The word *Iowa* has been interpreted to mean "beautiful land."

**Nickname:** Hawkeye State

**Capital:** Des Moines

**Motto:** Our Liberties We Prize, and Our Rights We Will Maintain

**Bird:** Eastern goldfinch

**Flower:** Wild prairie rose

**Tree:** Oak

**Rock:** Geode

*Goldfinch*

*Prairie rose*

# THE SONG OF IOWA

Iowa has no official state song, but "The Song of Iowa" has been accepted and sung as such since its composition by S.H.M. Byers in 1897. Its composer gave the following account of the inspiration for the song:

*At the great battle of Lookout Mountain [in Tennessee in 1863 during the Civil War] I was captured . . . and taken to Libby Prison, Richmond, Va. I was there seven months in one room. The rebel bands often passed the prison, and for our discomfiture, sometimes played the tune "Maryland, My Maryland," set to Southern and bitter words. Hearing it once through our barred windows, I said to myself, "I would like some day to put that tune to loyal words."*

**Words by S.H.M. Byers**

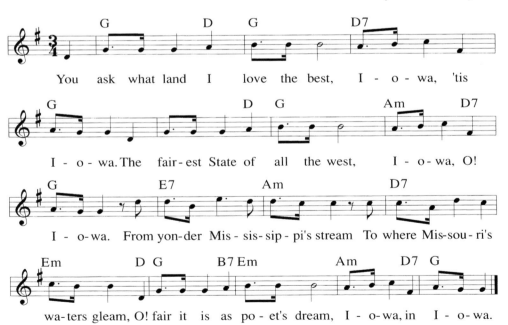

And she has maids whose laughing eyes,
Iowa, O! Iowa,
To him who loves were Paradise,
Iowa, O! Iowa.
O! happiest fate that e'er was known,
Such eyes to shine for one along.
To call such beauty all his own.
Iowa, O! Iowa.

See yonder fields of tasseled corn,
Iowa, in Iowa,
Where Plenty fills her golden horn,
Iowa, in Iowa.
See how her wondrous prairies shine
To yonder sunset's purpling line.
O! happy land, O! land of mine,
Iowa, O! Iowa

Go read the story of thy past,
Iowa, O! Iowa
What glorious deeds, what fame thou hast!
Iowa, O! Iowa
So long as time's great cycle runs,
Or nations weep their fallen sons,
Thou'lt not forget thy patriot sons,
Iowa, O! Iowa

# GEOGRAPHY

**Highest Point:** 1,670 feet, in northern Osceola County

**Lowest Point:** 480 feet, along the Mississippi and Des Moines rivers at Keokuk

**Area:** 56,275 square miles

**Greatest Distance North to South:** 214 miles

**Greatest Distance East to West:** 332 miles

**Bordering States:** Minnesota and South Dakota to the north, Wisconsin and Illinois to the east, Missouri to the south, and Nebraska and South Dakota to the west

**Hottest Recorded Temperature:** 118°F at Keokuk on July 20, 1934

**Coldest Recorded Temperature:** −47°F at Washta on January 12, 1912, and at Elkader on February 3, 1996

**Average Annual Precipitation:** 32 inches

**Major Rivers:** Big Sioux, Cedar, Chariton, Des Moines, Floyd, Iowa, Little Sioux, Maquoketa, Mississippi, Missouri, Nodaway, Skunk, Thompson, Wapsipinicon

**Major Lakes:** Clear, East Okoboji, Spirit, Storm, West Okoboji

**Trees:** ash, basswood, cedar, cottonwood, elm, hickory, maple, oak, walnut, willow

**Wild Plants:** aster, bloodroot, dog fennel, goldenrod, honeysuckle, mayapple, milkweed, prairie aster, prairie grass, prairie lily, rose, shooting star

*Goldenrod*

**Animals:** beaver, chipmunk, coyote, deer, fox, gopher, mink, muskrat, opossum, rabbit, raccoon, rattlesnake, squirrel, skunk

**Birds:** blue jay, Canada goose, cardinal, ducks, hawks, goldfinch, partridge, red-winged blackbird, robin, starling, tufted titmouse

**Fish:** bass, bluegill, carp, catfish, crappie, northern pike, perch, sucker, walleye

**Endangered Animals:** gray wolf, Indiana bat, Iowa snail, pearly mussel, piping plover, sturgeon

## TIMELINE

**Iowa History**

**c. 500** B.C.E. Mound Builders inhabit area.

**1300** C.E. The Oneota people move into what would become Iowa.

**1600s** Siouan ethnic groups, including Ioway, Omaha, Oto, Missouri, and Sioux (or Dakota) arrive in present-day Iowa.

**1673** French explorers Father Jacques Marquette and Louis Jolliet become the first known Europeans to see present-day Iowa.

**1733** Sauk and Fox Indians arrive in Iowa after being forced out of Wisconsin by the French.

**1788** Julien Dubuque, Iowa's first settler, begins mining land near present-day Dubuque.

*Piping plover*

**1803** United States acquires Iowa from France in the Louisiana Purchase.

**1808** The U.S. Army builds Fort Madison, the first U.S. military outpost in Iowa.

**1820** Congress passes the Missouri Compromise, which later made Iowa a free (nonslave) territory in 1838.

**1832** The U.S. Army defeats Sauk and Fox Indians led by Black Hawk in the Black Hawk War.

**1836** Congress creates the Territory of Wisconsin, which includes Iowa, Minnesota, and most of the Dakotas.

**1838** The Territory of Iowa is created.

**1846** Iowa becomes the twenty-ninth state.

**1857** The state legislature adopts Iowa's present constitution; the state capital moves to Des Moines.

**1867** The first railroad across Iowa is completed.

**1868** An amendment to the state constitution gives black males the right to vote.

**1869** Iowan Annabella Babbs Mansfield becomes first woman admitted to the practice of law in the United States.

**1913** Engineers complete the Keokuk Dam.

**1917** Iowa begins an extensive road-building program.

**1931** Iowan Susan Glaspell wins the Pulitzer Prize in drama for *Alison's House*.

**1953** State legislature creates a nine-member state board of education.

**1985** State lottery is established to raise revenue.

**1986** Justice Linda Neuman becomes the first woman to serve on the Iowa Supreme Court.

**1993** Heavy rains result in major floods, causing over $2 billion worth of damage.

**1999** Upon completing his fourth four-year term in office, Terry Branstad holds the record for the most years as Iowa's governor.

**2002** Iowa ranks fourth nationally on high school graduation rates at 84 percent.

**2004** Iowans witness a record number of tornadoes: 120.

**2005** Iowa is ranked as the sixth best state to live in; Iowa is ranked first in the nation for lands set aside to protect the environment through conservation (469,795 acres).

## ECONOMY

**Agricultural Products:** beef, chicken, corn, dairy products, hogs, soybeans, turkey

**Manufactured Products:** appliances, chemicals, electrical equipment, fabricated metal products, farm machinery, food products, furniture

**Natural Resources:** clay, coal, grade A soil, gypsum, limestone, sand

**Business and Trade:** communication, finance, insurance, real estate, retail trade, transportation, wholesale trade, bioscience

## CALENDAR OF CELEBRATIONS

**Sac City Kiwanis Kite Tournament** Kite-flying enthusiasts enjoy one of the country's oldest kiting tournaments here every spring. The Iowan sky is speckled with thousands of kites, ranging from homemade paper kites to high-tech dual-control featherweight stunt kites.

**Cedar Basin Jazz Festival** Tap your toes to the Dixieland bands that liven up this annual event held in Cedar Falls during the last weekend in June.

**Saturday in the Park** Fireworks aren't the only thing that brings a bang to Sioux City on the first Saturday in July. Music lovers get a special treat with a blues musicfest. Local and national talent provide the entertainment.

*Piglet*

**College Hill Arts Festival** Mid-July brings fabulous art to the University of Northern Iowa campus in Cedar Falls. More than seventy-five artists show their original works and offer demonstrations.

**RAGBRAI (***Register's* **Annual Great Bicycle Ride Across Iowa)** This touring bicycle ride celebrates Iowa's beautiful countryside during the last week of July. It attracts cyclists from all fifty states and several foreign countries. The route is never exactly the same, so many Iowa towns get the chance to open their homes to participants to make this a real statewide celebration.

**Nordic Fest** Decorah honors its Norwegian ancestors during this annual festival held the last weekend in July. Visitors can sample food, dances, and music for an authentic taste of Scandinavia. They can also enjoy exhibits on woodworking, Norwegian knife-making, rosemaling, and weaving. Children can enjoy storytellers and puppet shows.

**Tanager Place Summer Fest** Colorful hot-air balloons dot the Iowa sky during the first weekend in June. Rockwell Collins hosts this festival that also features family fun and entertainment and nonstop live music.

**Cedar Trails Festival** Thousands come to Cedar Valley in August to take special advantage of its more than 80 miles of beautiful recreational trails. Take a spin during the nighttime bike ride and enjoy a live music concert along the way.

**Holzfest** Families enjoy the Midwest's greatest wood show every August in the Amana Colonies. In addition to seeing woodworking displays, visitors can dance, listen to music, and enjoy the homemade food.

**Old Time Power Show** August is the time to revisit the pioneer settlement days in Cedar Falls. The city marks the end of summer with tractor pulls, parades, flea markets, and a display of antique farm equipment.

**Eulenspiegel Puppet Theatre** The only professional puppet troupe in Iowa brings folk and fairy tales to life at the Owl Glass Puppetry Center in West Liberty. Performances are offered between September and June.

### STATE STARS

**Adrian Constantine (Cap) Anson** (1851–1922) was known as the greatest baseball player of the nineteenth century. Born in Marshalltown, he led the Chicago White Stockings to five pennants and became the first major-league player to get three thousand hits.

**Leon Bismarck (Bix) Beiderbecke** (1903–1931) was an accomplished jazz musician who won acclaim during his short life. Born in Davenport, he won audiences' hearts with his cornet solos. During his career, he performed with many great jazz bands, but his peers regarded his small jazz combos as his greatest successes. Beiderbecke composed "Singin' the Blues" and "In a Mist."

**Black Hawk** (1767–1838) was a Sauk Indian leader who fought on the side of the British during the War of 1812. He believed his people had been tricked into ceding their lands east of the Mississippi River to the U.S. government and refused to move west of the Mississippi. He fought the Black Hawk War in 1832 to defend Indian lands but was defeated.

*Black Hawk*

**Amelia Jenks Bloomer** (1818–1894) advocated Prohibition and women's rights. As an adult, she settled in Council Bluffs, where she headed the Iowa Woman Suffrage Association. She popularized loose-fitting pants for women that came to be called "bloomers."

*Amelia Jenks Bloomer*

**Norman Ernest Borlaug** (1914–   ), who was born near Cresco, developed new varieties of wheat during his career as an agricultural scientist. In the 1950s and 1960s the wheat developed by Borlaug was introduced to India, Pakistan, and Mexico. He won the 1970 Nobel Peace Prize for his food production work. In addition to the Nobel Prize, Borlaug has also received the 2002 Public Welfare Medal from the U.S. National Academy of Sciences; the Padma Vibhushan, India's second-highest civilian award in 2006; and the 2004 National Medal of Science, the highest scientific honor of the United States, from U.S. President George W. Bush on November 14, 2005.

**Johnny Carson** (1925–2005) was a popular entertainer who hosted *The Tonight Show* for thirty years. His success as a talk-show host has been attributed to his easygoing manner and ability to get people to talk about themselves. He was born in Corning.

**Carrie Chapman Catt** (1859–1947) helped form the Iowa Woman Suffrage Association. An educator as well as social reformer, she served as principal and superintendent of Mason City schools. She led the campaign that resulted in the ratification of the Nineteenth Amendment to the U.S. Constitution in 1920, which gave women the right to vote.

**Lee de Forest** (1873–1961), an inventor born in Council Bluffs, was known as the Father of Radio because he created transmitting and receiving devices. He equipped U.S. Navy ships with wireless telephones and inaugurated radio news broadcasts.

**George Gallup** (1901–1984) was a public-opinion expert. Born in Jefferson, he founded the American Institute of Public Opinion, which conducted the famous Gallup Poll.

**Hamlin Garland** (1860–1940) grew up facing the hardships of pioneer life on the Iowa frontier and turned his experiences into widely read books. He wrote *Main-Travelled Roads* and *A Son of the Middle Border*, which was his autobiography. In 1922 he won the Pulitzer Prize in biography for *A Daughter of the Middle Border*.

**Susan Glaspell** (1882–1948) was born in Davenport. She and her husband founded the prestigious Provincetown Playhouse. A novelist and playwright, she won the 1930 Pulitzer Prize in drama for *Alison's House*.

**Fred Grandy** (1948–    ), who was born in Sioux City, played Gopher on the television series *The Love Boat*. He entered politics in the mid-1980s and began his first term in the U.S. House of Representatives in 1987.

*Carrie Chapman Catt*

**Herbert Clark Hoover** (1874–1964) was president of the United States from 1929 to 1933. He earned a fortune as a geologist and mining engineer and then entered public service. Hoover served as head of the American Relief Commission in London and the Commission for Relief in Belgium during World War I. Prior to being elected president, this West Branch native served as secretary of commerce under President Calvin Coolidge.

**Glenn Miller** (1904–1944) was a bandleader who headed one of the most famous big bands. Born in Clarinda, he composed many famous songs, including "In the Mood," "Tuxedo Junction," "Little Brown Jug," and "Moonlight Serenade."

**Alfred** (1861–1919), **Charles** (1863–1926), and **John** (1866–1936) **Ringling**, who organized and founded the Ringling Brothers Circus, were born in MacGregor. They combined their circus with the Barnum and Bailey Circus to form the "Greatest Show on Earth."

**James Alfred Van Allen** (1914–    ), who was born in Mount Pleasant, headed the department of physics and astronomy at the University of Iowa for more than thirty years. His cosmic ray detection device discovered the two radiation belts around the Earth that are now called the Van Allen belts.

**Henry Agard Wallace** (1888–1965) was born in Adair County and gained prominence for helping farmers by popularizing the hardier and more productive hybrid corn seed. He served as secretary of agriculture and vice president under President Franklin Roosevelt. He was one of the most important figures of the New Deal period, promoting such controversial programs as paying farmers not to grow crops.

*Herbert Clark Hoover*

**Meredith Willson** (1902–1984) wrote the famous Broadway musical *The Music Man*. Willson used his hometown of Mason City as a basis for the fictional River City, Iowa, in the musical.

**Garfield Arthur Wood** (1880–1971) devised the PT boat used in World War II. This sportsman and industrialist from Mapleton also set world records in speedboat and hydroplane racing.

**Grant Wood** (1892–1942) portrayed the Midwest in his realistic paintings. His best-known work, *American Gothic*, features a midwestern man and his daughter. He was born in Anamosa.

## TOUR THE STATE

**Amana Colonies** Seven quaint villages rest in the lush Iowa River valley 20 miles southwest of Cedar Rapids. Once run by a communal religious society, the area is now a 26,000-acre national historic landmark. The heritage of the German settlers remains active, as residents still produce high-quality products, including food, furniture, and appliances. Visitors can watch the craftworkers build furniture and weave fabrics.

**Boone and Scenic Valley Railroad** Enjoy a taste of the transportation of yesteryear. This railroad takes travelers through Iowa's scenic countryside and over one of the highest bridges in the United States.

**Danish Windmill** See an authentic windmill from Denmark. Built in 1848 the windmill was dismantled, shipped to Iowa, and then rebuilt on its present site at Elk Horn.

*Danish Windmill*

**DeSoto National Wildlife Refuge** Visitors come here in the spring and fall to see thousands of duck and geese as they migrate through the Missouri River Valley. The visitors' center features wildlife exhibits and artifacts from the sunken steamboat *The Bertrand*.

**Effigy Mounds National Monument** At this site you can see the artifacts from Iowa's prehistoric Indian population. These effigy mounds near McGregor are in the shapes of birds and bears.

**Herbert Hoover National Historic Site** The white cottage in West Branch where Herbert Hoover was born is surrounded by a beautiful park. A restored blacksmith shop and the Herbert Hoover Presidential Library and Museum, which holds Hoover's public papers, are also there. Hoover was buried at the site in 1964.

**Living History Farms** Visitors can walk from the present to the past and back on these farms in Des Moines. This large open-air museum depicts Iowa farm life from pioneer days to the present. Costumed guides demonstrate skills and crafts on period farms.

**Paddlewheel Riverboat** You can enjoy fine dining and family entertainment while cruising on a Mississippi riverboat. Visitors take an interesting passage through the Mississippi's lock and dam system.

**Vesterheim Norwegian-American Museum** As you walk through these sixteen historic buildings that cover nearly a city block, you are seeing the most comprehensive collection of artifacts devoted

*Living History Farms*

to a single immigrant ethnic group in America. Norwegian Americans began collecting objects in the 1870s so they could preserve their history. More than 24,000 objects are housed at this site in Decorah, including a horse-head bowl dating from 1816 and an authentic interior of a log house built in 1850.

**Iowa Firefighters Memorial** This memorial honors the sacrifices made by Iowan firefighters. Located in Coralville, the memorial has a bronze statue of a firefighter rescuing a child. A granite wall bears the names of the professional and volunteer firefighters for whom the memorial was created.

**University of Iowa Museum of Natural History** Learn more about the natural world and its inhabitants in the second-oldest museum west of the Mississippi. The University of Iowa Museum features fascinating dioramas, including orangutans in a Borneo jungle and a walrus collected by Arctic explorer Robert Peary. The Iowa Hall gallery features a life-size giant Ice Age sloth among its many Iowa fossils.

**Devonian Fossil Gorge** The massive floods of 1993 eroded a 15-foot-deep channel exposing the underlying Devonian Age seafloor. Visitors can see ancient fossils and exposed rocks from Iowa's geologic past.

**University of Iowa Museum of Art** The centerpiece of this museum is one of the nation's most important collections of African sculpture. Changing exhibitions and selections from among the museum's approximately 12,000 works of art delight visitors year-round.

*Iowa Firefighters Memorial*

**Laura Ingalls Wilder Park and Museum** One of the childhood homes of this popular writer is found 12 miles north of Decorah. The house is furnished with period pieces that give visitors a look at the circumstances of Wilder's early years.

**Locust School** This historic schoolhouse 10 miles north of Decorah was built in 1854 and operated for 106 years.

**Black Hawk Park** There's plenty to do at this 1,490-acre park in Cedar Falls. You can camp, enjoy hiking trails, or practice your aim on the rifle and archery ranges.

**Loess Hills** In western Iowa, along the bluffs that border the Missouri Valley, is a dramatic natural landmark that spans nearly 10,000 acres. Loess is a common geologic material found in the Midwest. Here the loess reaches several hundred feet thick and is the dominant element of the terrain.

### FUN FACTS

The Pottawattamie County Jail in Council Bluffs was called the "Squirrel Cage Jail." Pie-shaped jail cells rotated around a central core. Once a prisoner entered a cell from the core, the cell was rotated to seal it off. In use from 1885 to 1969, the jail has been restored and is now open to the public.

Dubuque is home to the shortest, steepest operating railroad in the United States. The track is 296 feet long and rises at a 60-degree incline to a height of 189 feet.

*Loess Hills*

The Red Delicious apple was developed near East Peru. Originally called the "Hawkeye apple" when Jesse Hiatt entered it in an apple contest, it was renamed when the Stark Brothers Nursery purchased the rights to the fruit.

*Red Delicious apples*

# Find Out More

If you'd like to find out more about Iowa, check your local library or bookstore for these titles:

### GENERAL STATE BOOKS

Balcavage, Dynise. *Iowa.* Danbury, CT: Children's Press, 2002.

Christian, Sandra J. *Iowa.* Mankato, MN: Capstone Press, 2003.

Horton, Loren N. *Uniquely Iowa.* Chicago: Heinemann Library, 2004.

Smolen, Rick, and David Elliot Cohen. *Iowa: 24/7.* New York: DK Publishing, 2004.

### BOOKS OF SPECIAL INTEREST

Kule, Elaine A. *Iowa Facts and Symbols.* Mankato, MN: Capstone Press, 2003.

Thompson, Bill. *Iowa Bird Watching: A Year Round Guide.* Nashville, TN: Cool Springs Press, 2005.

Walters, Lynn L. *Great Iowa Walks: 50 Strolls, Hikes, and Treks.* Black Earth, WS: Trails Books, 2005.

## FICTION

Drury, Tom. *Hunts in Dreams*. Boston: Houghton Mifflin, 2002.

Garlock, Dorothy. *More than Memory*. New York: Warner Books, 2001.

McCutchen H.L. *Lightland*. New York: Orchard Books, 2002.

## WEB SITES

**Official State of Iowa Website**

http://www.iowa.gov

This site provides information on government, business, education, and tourism, and also contains links to many sites with details on all aspects of the Hawkeye State.

**Ioway Cultural Institute**

http://ioway.nativeweb.org/culture/ancestrallife.htm

At this site you will find information about the Ioway Native Americans, some of the first people to live in what is now the state of Iowa.

**World Almanac, Iowa**

http://www.worldalmanacforkids.com/explore/states/iowa.html

Visit this site for fun facts about Iowa, from geography to history.

**Iowa Pathways**

http://www.iptv.org/iowapathways/

To learn more about the people and the places in Iowa, try this Web site where you will see pictures of ancient artifacts, find a historic timeline, and even get a chance to create your own story about Iowa.

# Index

Page numbers in **boldface** are illustrations and charts.

Polly Morrice received her B.A. from Grinnell College in Grinnell, Iowa, where she drove through her first Iowa blizzard and learned that the best home-cooked meals are found in the Amana Colonies. She earned her M.A. from Yale University. A freelance writer and editor, she has published short fiction, magazine articles, essays, book reviews, and two nonfiction books for young readers.

Joyce Hart grew up on the East Coast, in big cities such as Washington, D.C., Charleston, South Carolina, and Orlando, Florida. She traveled a lot with her family, driving from the East Coast to the West Coast for summer vacations. She was always impressed by the wide open fields, the feeling of tightly knit, small communities, and the summer storms that brewed on the midwestern horizon as she and her family drove through states such as Iowa.

As an adult, Hart has sought out small communities in which to live. Today she lives in Hansville, Washington, a small, out-of-the-way place that no one seems to have heard of. There she writes books and edits other writers' work. At night she likes to go outside and search the skies for the Milky Way.